In The Presence Of Angels

A collection of inspiring, true angel stories

E. Lonnie Melashenko and Timothy E. Crosby

Pacific Press® Publishing Association
Nampa, Idaho
Oshawa, Ontario, Canada

Edited by Kenneth R. Wade
Designed by Dennis Ferree
Cover illustration by Miyuki Sena
Typeset in Esprit 11/13

Unless otherwise noted, all Scripture quotations are taken from the New International Version.

Melashenko, E. Lonnie.
    In the presence of angels : a collection of inspiring, true angel stories /E. Lonnie Melashenko and Timothy E. Crosby.
        p.   cm.
    ISBN 0-8163-1261-3 (pbk. : alk. paper)
    1. Angels—Case studies. I. Crosby, Timothy E., 1954- .
II. Title.
BT966.2.M37 1995
235'.3—dc20   95-6966
                                                         CIP

97 98 99 00 01 ● 10 9 8 7

Contents

A rumor of angels; a rustle of wings,
The sound of the song that a seraph sings,
Then silence—and no one for sure could say
But it may be that God was here today.

—Tim Crosby

CHAPTER

1

The Argument for Angels

You've probably never seen an angel. Perhaps none of your friends have seen an angel. You've probably never seen the North Pole either. But you don't doubt that it's there, do you? Even the handful of men who have been to the pole saw nothing but endless snow. Yet no one doubts that it exists.

There are many more people alive today who have seen angels than have seen the North Pole. This book is full of their stories.

Angels are not mythical creatures, psychological

projections of human emotions, wish fulfillments, imaginary personifications of virtues, or figments of fertile imaginations. Nor are they reincarnated humans who have moved on to a higher level. They are real, created beings who exist in the realm of the spirit. They laugh, they cry, they love, they worship, and they sometimes interfere in human affairs.

There are many things in our world that are invisible, yet real. Take one of the most common of all substances—water. At this very moment, unseen gallons of water are floating in the air around you. Change the temperature and pressure a little, and this unseen gas becomes a liquid. We can drink it, swim in it, float ships in it. Change the temperature still more, and it becomes solid. But it is no less real when it is invisible than when it is visible.

We now know that most things in our universe have a much higher degree of hiddenness than water vapor.

Those who doubt the reality of a spirit world may be unaware of something that physicists have recently come to understand: Most of the matter in the universe is intangible to us—not merely invisible, but completely undetectable. We know it's there, but so far we have been unable to find it. Frank Wilczek explains:

> One of the most frustrating of our unsolved problems is the missing-mass phenomenon. There are compelling reasons, both theoretical and observational, to believe that most of the mass of the universe is quite unlike anything astronomers have seen so far. The density of the universe, as inferred from the strength of the gravitational pull of one portion on another, is at least ten times what can be accounted for by adding up all known sources. The remainder, the so-called missing mass, or "dark matter" (which is actually not dark but transparent), cannot be planets, gas clouds, or anything of a familiar sort. Indeed, the dark matter almost surely cannot be anything assembled from the conventional building blocks of matter—protons,

neutrons, and electrons—in any way whatsoever.[1]

Consider our awesome ignorance: we do not even know what 90 percent of the universe is made of! A bit of intellectual humility, then, is in order. We must allow for the possibility that angels might be made of the same exotic matter that constitutes this missing mass. Perhaps heaven itself is composed of this invisible matter and exists all around us, in another dimension. Such speculation is no longer metaphysical jabberwocky; it now fits into the scheme of modern physics.

Why do we tend to believe physicists? Many people believe in atoms and black holes, though no one has ever seen either, because physicists tell us they are implied by their equations.

One reason for our faith in physics is that it is based on experimental evidence. By the same token, we have tried to provide evidence for angels in the pages of this book, showing the results of the experiment of prayer. However, there is another factor. While faith in the physicists costs us nothing, a belief in the supernatural is expensive because of the life-changing implications. If the Bible is right about angels, then maybe it is also right about God, and maybe there is a judgment after all. And a heaven. And a hell.

Thousands of people have seen angels, while no one has ever seen atoms or black holes. So why are there so many religious skeptics?

Could it be because human beings tend to ignore that which costs too much to believe?

Most older, well-educated people tend to believe only that which they or someone they know has experienced. In other words, if it's never happened to anyone they know of, it probably doesn't happen. The more highly educated a person is, the more likely they are to think this way.

An extreme example of this would be the prolific writer Isaac Asimov. Author of five hundred books, with an encyclopedic knowledge of the physical world, Asimov did not believe in the supernatural.

IN THE PRESENCE OF ANGELS

Yet Asimov himself would be the first to admit that he knew only a small fraction of all there was to know about the universe. For the sake of argument, let's say he knew one-tenth of all there was to know (a very generous supposition). Is it not quite possible, then, that angels exist outside Asimov's domain of knowledge—somewhere in the remaining 90 percent?

The fact is that people like Asimov start out with certain presuppositions that cause them to routinely discard evidence of the kind found in these pages. Perceptions are filtered by presuppositions: the sort of evidence a person accepts is largely determined by one's cultural community. Once our belief system is formed, we tend to ignore evidence that does not fit into the system, just as we avoid buying furniture that will not fit into our living room. Buying a new house just to fit the furniture is just too expensive.

Likewise, most people avoid new ideas that require major renovation of their belief system. But what if there is compelling evidence supporting these new ideas? Would you be willing to pursue truth, whatever the cost?

In these pages you will find substantial evidence that angels are real. If you are a skeptic, you must supply the willingness to believe, whatever the cost. Anyone willing to pay the price will find himself living in a much larger household, with many new brothers and sisters, more room to grow, and indeed,

> More sky than he can see,
> More seas than he can sail,
> More sun than he can bear to watch,
> More stars than he can scale.
> More breath than he can breathe,
> More yield than he can sow.
> More grace than he can comprehend.
> More love than he can know!
> —Ralph W. Seager.

To an intelligent skeptic, the most obvious explanation of angel sightings is the psychological one: it's all in the mind. Angel visions are hallucinations; perhaps some sort of mental defense mechanism in reaction to intense fear and stress.

Two things rule out this explanation. First, there are the physical effects: the fixed car, the bag of groceries, the healing, the ride home. Second, sometimes the angel is seen, not by the endangered narrator, but by a third party, as in the following story given to me by Skye Heatherton-East, the daughter of Dr. Charles and Florence Duggie. Incidentally, in many of the stories, we have identified the people involved by first name and last initial only, to protect their privacy; however, we have supplied the full name in stories that have been published before and in cases in which the author has given us permission to do so.

About 1983 Dr. and Mrs. Duggie were traveling from northern California to their home near Los Angeles. About 1:00 in the morning, they were running low on gasoline and pulled off into the city of Oakland. Finding a gas station open in a rundown part of town, they pulled in. Five or six rough-looking men who were standing and talking stopped and began to look over their car. The Duggies felt vulnerable and prayed for protection. As the gas transaction was completed, the attendant asked them where they had picked up the two marines in the back seat.

This was a bit of a jolt to the Duggies, because they hadn't picked up anybody. Nevertheless, they didn't look into the back seat until they were on the road. When they turned around, no one was there. There was nothing left to do but thank God for His protection.

Here are two more such stories.

IN THE PRESENCE OF ANGELS

Last summer a friend and I were selling religious books in the southwestern part of Fresno, California.

Many of the interests we met were individuals who wanted us to come back the following day. My partner couldn't be with me the following day, so I had to follow up the interests alone.

The next day I called back on two customers and made two sales; one was a time payment order, while the other was a cash order for a large set of books.

The cash sale was in the evening, and I had parked my car about one block from the customer's house.

As I left the house, I noticed several individuals near my car. I had the funny feeling that they were waiting for me, so I looked up and down the street to see if there were other people about, but there were none.

I stopped and offered a short prayer asking for divine protection, and I felt immediate peace.

As I started to walk to my car, someone from behind said, "I'll walk you to your car." I was taken aback, for I hadn't noticed anyone near me. The three men never moved from my car. One of them had a wooden handle with a chain attached to it.

I unlocked my car, got in, and started up my motor. I looked about to thank the stranger, but he was nowhere in sight. I drove up the street and turned around and came back to see if I could find the stranger. He was nowhere to be seen. I thanked the Lord for His protection and the stranger befriending me.

I had a sales referral from that last customer, but because it was after dark, I felt it would be best to return the next morning.

The next day I called on the referral and sold her the same set of books. She lived on the same street as the woman who had given me the referral, not far from the place where I had parked my car the night before. My customer of the day before had called her friend on the phone and told her I might come to see her the same evening, so she was at the window watching me go to my car. She also noticed the three men near my car and, knowing they were up to no good, she started to pray for me that nothing would happen. She also noticed someone walking beside me from the time I left her friend's house to my car. She saw the man get into the passenger side before I drove off.

I could only conclude that my angel was protecting me that evening, and this woman was allowed to see all the evidence for some special reason.

—Jim Hartwick.[2]

At five o'clock in the morning, I was awakened by the loud clanging of a prayer bell. The idea of praying seemed like a good one, so I rolled out of bed and began.

"Dear God," I prayed, "I'm afraid of being here in this city. I need protection that only You can give. I know that You have sent angels to be with those who love You. I could use that kind of protection today. And if You don't mind, send me two angels."

Soon I was on the streets of Belize. As I headed to the restaurant for breakfast, the people stood back and stared as I passed by them. I chose a table, and a stranger seated himself at my table. He introduced himself as Timothy and asked me to buy him a cup of coffee. I made the order; then Tim and I began talking. After a few moments, Tim looked at me intently and asked, "Who were those two men you were with this morning?"

I nearly choked on my orange juice. "You saw me with two men this morning?"

"Yes," he answered. "Who were they?"

"Tim," I questioned, "are you sure it was me you saw?"

"Yes, it was you!" he replied, a bit annoyed that I was avoiding his question. "I saw you walking up the street with two men. Was one of them your father?"

11

I hesitated. "No, neither of them was my father."

Tim seemed satisfied with my answer and did not question me further. However, as I finished my meal, I wondered if those men had come from my Father—my heavenly Father. When I had prayed earlier that morning for protection, I had been confident that God would protect me. Why was I so surprised that God had answered my prayer in the way I had asked?

After finishing my meal, I returned to the streets of Belize City. This time I was filled with peace rather than fear. I looked at all those blank staring faces, and I couldn't help wondering, *Do those people see one man, or three?*

—David George.[3]

At this point Occam's razor comes in handy. A swift incision with this logical tool will prevent us from multiplying ingenious theories unnecessarily. The simplest explanation of these and the rest of the stories in this book is the traditional one.

However, to be fair, the traditional position raises questions that are difficult to answer. One of the most difficult questions raised by angel stories is this: why do they happen so rarely? For every miracle story in this book, there are hundreds of other instances in which God chose not to intervene. Why?

We will return to this question at several points throughout the book. No one knows the full answer. But we can nibble around its edges.

Suppose you were the chief executive officer of a large corporation, and you hired your son to work in the mailroom. As your son worked his way up through the ranks, he sometimes ran into trouble. Whenever he did, he would ask you to pull strings and solve problems for him that he could solve for himself if he tried a little harder. What would you do? Would you bail him out of every trouble? Would you really be helping him if you pulled strings so he could get whatever he wanted? Would this produce a resourceful, responsible son who could be entrusted to management someday?

One reason, then, that God does not save His children from all danger is that we need the growth more than we need the protection. A moderate amount of suffering seasons us. In fact, pain is something of a shortcut to spiritual maturity; it puts us on God's fast track.

The job of a guardian angel is not to make our life free of all unpleasantness but to protect us from *spiritual* danger. This may mean at times allowing us to experience physical pain while strengthening us to bear it. After all, the servant is not greater than his Master. When Jesus prayed for His Father to keep Him from the cross, God's only answer was to send an angel to strengthen Him (see Luke 22:42, 43). Many of the greatest saints mentioned in the Bible were not delivered from suffering and death.

Like a good parent, God does not always protect His children from the consequences of their deeds or bail them out of every inconvenience. The quick fix is not usually the best. God is more interested in our future glory than our present comfort.

This is not by any means a complete answer. The problem of the rarity of miracles and the abundance of suffering is perhaps humankind's greatest philosophical problem. Why is God silent? We find the following analogy helpful in understanding this mystery.

Psychologists once conducted a now-famous experiment in which unsuspecting subjects were recruited to administer electric shocks to a person sitting on the other side of a glass partition. The person who was supposedly being shocked was in fact an actor who only pretended to feel the pain, using appropriate grimaces, shrieks, etc. The unsuspecting subjects of the experiment controlled a lever that went from mild shock to something like "Extremely Painful and Dangerous." During the experiment, each subject was eventually asked to increase the level of pain to its maximum. All but a few subjects complied.

In another experiment, subjects were asked to tell which of several straws was the longest, along with a room full of other people. The unsuspecting subjects did not know that the rest of the people in the room had been instructed to choose the wrong straw. Even though the correct answer was obvious, most subjects were unable to resist peer pressure. They also chose the wrong straw.

We do not wish to discuss the psychological implications of these experiments but to draw an analogy between them and the precarious situation in which humankind finds itself on planet Earth.

Notice two things about these experiments. First, many subjects were no doubt thinking, *Something's not quite right here.* The "strangeness" of the experiment raised questions that remained unanswered until they were let in on the secret.

Secondly, only a few of the subjects were able to resist and do the "right" thing.

The Bible portrays God as occasionally conducting such experiments on a smaller scale. For example, 2 Chronicles 32:31 says that when emissaries came to inquire of Hezekiah, God left him to himself as a test to see what he would do. Similar experiments are mentioned in Exodus 16:4, Deuteronomy 8:2, Judges 2:22, 3:1-4, 1 Kings 22:19-23, and, most significantly, the book of Job.

We would like to suggest that, like Job of old, we are all subjects in a grand experiment, initiated by Satan, but allowed by God. This earth is a cosmic laboratory for the benefit of unseen intelligences. As in the case of Job, *we are not being told all the facts*—this is essential to the success of the experiment; just as in double-blind experiments today.

The "strangeness" of our world is due to the artificial constructs of the experiment. And as in the experiments mentioned above, doing the "right" thing is uncommon, requiring a degree of resistance to the pressure of the norm.

Other than the first two fascinating chapters of the book of Job in the Old Testament (which you should read if you're interested in knowing what's going on behind the scenes in our world), there are several passages in the New Testament that support the idea that we are subjects of a grand experiment, whose results are of interest to angels:

> For it seems to me that God has put us apostles on display at the end of the procession, like men condemned to die in the arena. We have been made a spectacle to the whole universe, to angels as well as to men (1 Corinthians 4:9).

> His intent was that now, through the church, the manifold wisdom of God should be made known to the rulers and authorities in the heavenly realms (Ephesians 3:10).

Holy angels are students of God's plan for our planet; they are watching us with deep interest. "Even angels," writes Peter, "long to look into these things" (1 Peter 1:12). Mind-boggling as it seems, angels have something to learn from us.

This provides an answer of sorts to the greatest philosophical question of all time: "Why does a God who is both good and all-powerful allow evil?" The answer: "It only works that way for now, in the laboratory. We'll find out why as soon as the experiment is over. Then it will all make sense." If something's not quite right here, there's a reason for it. While God does not *will* evil, He tolerates it for some greater good that is only partly apparent to us now.

For now, we must be content to trust the Director of the laboratory. He cannot allow His angels to intervene very often; that would compromise the Experiment. But once in a while He does, just to let us know He's there, watching out for us.

It seems that one of the questions to be answered in this great experiment has to do with the nature of love and loyalty. Can God's creatures love Him for Himself alone, apart from the benefits, or

15

do we serve Him only to get His blessings?

This requires that miracles be allotted sparingly. After all, if becoming a Christian meant automatic protection from all evil, then what would happen? Wouldn't we start to take God for granted? Would not the entire world become nominally Christian, not out of love for God but out of love for His powers?

Miracles are elusive. There are only about forty recorded in the Bible, spread over a span of several thousand years. And even these miracles are not randomly distributed. They tend to cluster around great events in salvation history and to be associated with specific prophets: Moses and his successor Joshua, Elijah and his successor Elisha, and Jesus and His successors the apostles.

Even the apostles, however, could not always work miracles consistently. When Paul wrote to the Romans and Corinthians, he reminded them of the signs and wonders and miracles that he had worked among them as signs of his apostolic authority (see Romans 15:19; 2 Corinthians 12:12). But by the time he wrote 2 Timothy, his last book, he could not even heal his own coworker Trophimus, whom he had to leave sick at Miletus (4:20).

True miracles tend to occur in primitive areas where the power of Satan is manifest and wherever God is beginning a new work. At such times, miracles are needed to establish faith. As the work is established and the faith of the new believers grows to maturity, the miracles typically taper off. The children must believe based on the testimony of the fathers.

Jesus Himself, the greatest miracle worker of all time, seemed to disparage miracles. To doubting Thomas, Jesus said, "Blessed are those who have not seen and yet have believed" (John 20:29). He labeled those who demanded a miracle "wicked and adulterous" (Matthew 12:38, 39), and He taught that even false prophets can work real miracles (see Matthew 7:15-23).

The Bible makes it clear that miracles are not necessarily signs of righteousness or holiness, as illustrated by a comparison between John the Baptist and Judas. John the Baptist did not work any miracles (see John 10:41, 42), yet Jesus spoke highly of him as "more than a prophet" (Matthew 11:9) and said of him, "Among those born of women there has not risen anyone greater than John the Baptist" (verse 11). Judas, on the other hand, was given authority "to drive out all demons and to cure diseases," along with the rest of the apostles (Luke 9:1). Although the miracles he worked were a genuine gift, yet Jesus called him a devil and "the one doomed to destruction" (John 17:12).

Rasputin, the monk who did so much evil in the last days of the Russian monarchy, was well known for his miracles.

In other words, miracles can be dangerous and may prove nothing. They can be used by both sides. When Moses worked miracles before Pharaoh, Pharaoh's pagan priests duplicated several of them (see Exodus 7:10-12). Finally, whenever the New Testament mentions miracles in the last days, they are always false miracles (see Matthew 24:24; 2 Thessalonians 2:9-12; Revelation 16:14).

It is dangerous, then, to trust in miracles, because miracles are a trademark of the dark powers near the end of time. Perhaps it is because of this possibility of counterfeit that God rarely uses supernatural means to accomplish what could be done by natural means.

Nevertheless, the counterfeit implies the presence of the real thing. Jesus predicted that miracles would accompany the preaching of His message (see Mark 16:17, 18; John 14:12), and they still do—perhaps more frequently than ever. The most unlikely people suddenly find themselves in the presence of angels. We have been privileged to collect their stories, just as the disciples gathered the fragments after Jesus miraculously fed the five thousand, that others might share their wonder.

However, one has to be careful to sort the good from the bad. We have no desire to foster new urban legends.

Urban legends are sensational stories that have persisted over time and achieved wide circulation. Christian urban legends tend to offer miraculous support for some article of faith. One of the most persis-

17

tent is the decades-old story of the vanishing hitchhiker.

A man is driving along a highway. He offers a ride to a hitch-hiker, who tells him that Jesus is coming very soon. Suddenly, the hitchhiker disappears from inside the moving vehicle. The driver pulls into a police station and tells his story, whereupon he is told that seven other motorists have told the same story that day.

This story has gone around the world several times. However, no one has ever been able to trace it to its origin. It always happened to "a friend of a friend." And so, until someone can pin it down to a time, place, and person, it will continue to be a legend.

We have tried to avoid such stories. Most of the stories in this book are first-person accounts, told by the person who had the experience. Even the stories that are narrated in the third person came to us, for the most part, as first-person accounts that we adapted for stylistic variety. In a few cases we have used stories in which the writer describes an experience that happened to a named friend. But for the most part, we have avoided secondhand stories.

For quite a few years, the "Voice of Prophecy" radio broadcast has averaged about one series a year on angels. Since 1990 we have, over the air, invited our listeners to write us with any angel experiences they have had, indicating that we might use some of them on the air or in this book. For every letter reproduced here, we have received two or three others that we could not use. The letters in this volume have undergone minor editing for grammar and felicity of expression. In no case have we ever intentionally changed the thought. We owe a debt of gratitude to the writers who have been so kind as to let us use their stories.

We hope any angels who might be looking over our shoulders are not unhappy about what we have said about them and that the reader might be led to a love of the One they so tirelessly serve.

---

1. Frank Wilczek, "The End of Physics?" *Discover*, March 1993.
2. *Pacific Union Recorder,* 2 July 1990, 2.
3. "Alone in Belize City," *Insight,* 8 March 1986.

CHAPTER

2

The Shelter of His Wings

It was a letter dated July 23, 1990, that rekindled our interest in angels at the "Voice of Prophecy," and eventually resulted in the publication of this book. Here is what it said:

Dear Pastor Richards:

I hear you over WWJC Duluth and enjoy your program. Have you talked about the work and power of angels?

I had the wonderful experience of seeing one once

in my bedroom. I was caring for some children in a home one night. I felt someone lovingly caressing me, and thinking it one of the children, suggested she return to bed. I had not opened my eyes while talking, but as no one answered I did, and there stood a beautiful angel by my bed! I remember the wings came about to the knees and to the sides of its body. Then the angel vanished from my sight!

—Ruby W., Aitkin, Minnesota.

Do angels have wings? When God authorized Moses to create a golden throne on top of the ark that held a copy of His holy law, He told him to place two cherubim (angels) above it, facing each other, with their wings spread over it (see Exodus 25:20; 37:9). When Solomon built his temple, he also placed winged cherubim in the Most Holy Place with their wings spread over the ark of the covenant (see 1 Kings 6:27; 8:6, 7; 1 Chronicles 28:18; 2 Chronicles 3:13; 5:7, 8). The seraphs Isaiah saw in vision had six wings (see Isaiah 6:2), while Ezekiel, in chapter 1 of his book, describes in some detail a class of glorious "living creatures" who had four wings. In chapter 10 these creatures are described further and are called "cherubs" (*cherubs* is the English equivalent to the Hebrew *cherubim*; in Hebrew the plural is created by adding *im* to the end of a word). Revelation 4:8 talks about four living creatures with six wings, covered with eyes (like peacock feathers?), who stand around the throne of God crying, "Holy, holy, holy is the Lord God Almighty, who was, and is, and is to come."

However, "angels" in the Bible are never said to have wings. They always appear in the form of men. Only cherubs and seraphs have wings. However, these have traditionally been regarded as types of angels.

God is also mentioned as having wings in Scripture, but these appear to be metaphorical, like the expression "wings of the wind" (Psalm 18:10) or "wings of the dawn" (Psalm 139:9).

Actually, God's "wings" seem to be more of an instrument of comfort and protection than an instrument of flight; they are something under which His children may take refuge:

> Have mercy on me, O God, have mercy on me, for in you my soul takes refuge. I will take refuge in the shadow of your wings until the disaster has passed (Psalm 57:1).

> You yourselves have seen . . . how I carried you on eagles' wings and brought you to myself (Exodus 19:4).[1]

Perhaps that is also the intent of angelic wings, for winged angels usually appear in modern times to those who need comfort and encouragement. Here are four accounts of people who have seen angel wings and who have discovered what the psalmist must have felt when he said, "Because you are my help, I sing in the shadow of your wings" (Psalm 63:7).

Connie P., of Vinita, Oklahoma, had been preparing for baptism, and she was filled with joy as new insights filled her mind and heart. She was baptized with a deep love for the Lord.

During this time, Satan saw to it that there was an immense problem plaguing her almost daily. Her husband, an alcoholic, was bitterly opposed to the new direction her life was taking. He worked earnestly to draw her children away from God. The emotional stress was overwhelming, and the situation was growing worse day by day.

One evening she dozed off and then was suddenly awakened. There in the corner of her bedroom was the most beautiful being she had ever seen. It appeared to be an angel of a pale grayish color. Connie had not studied about angels yet and did not even think of them as possessing "real wings." The vision was from the shoulder to the waist. His robe was draped down his side and from his bent forearm.

The figure was of stately stature. Connie could see one wing, but it was *very* large and looked tremendously powerful. It gave the appearance of a regular feathered bird wing. In comparison with the body, the wing was immense in size. Connie writes:

> I was honored to have this vision for approximately four to six seconds. Of course, I do not know, but I believe this was my guardian angel. Even if it was another angel, I know that God sent the vision to me for strength and comfort. Once you have experienced such a privilege, it makes our God and all of heaven very real—not just an abstraction.

Roberta Z., of Newfield, Maine, found herself unemployed and discouraged. She writes:

> I have had sole custody of my children for over ten years. At times it has been rewarding; sometimes devastating. Unfortunately, my walk has been without the support of many others, living in a world where friends are too busy to really lend an ear.
>
> I have supported my family for over a year now on only $150.00 per week, trying to find a way out of this.
>
> I had become very weary, drained, and without hope. I had just about lost hope in everyone and everything. Being a Christian, I lean on my faith, but even God's Word was not lifting me out of my slump.
>
> This past Memorial Day weekend was like many others, and I struggled to get through the holiday. A few close friends lent what support they could, and I felt a bit better. Toward the end of the holiday, one of my children had an accident that required a trip to the hospital. We started for home close to midnight.
>
> As I drove, I remembered the many times I had made this trip in the past. I heard a gentle voice speak in my mind, telling me that I had so much to be proud of and that I had done what many find difficult even with the help of another parent.

I gazed at my child, who was resting and felt an incredible amount of love and peace. I felt very happy and sure that my future would be brighter, which was in contrast to the hopelessness I had felt over the weekend. What I experienced over the next five minutes explains where this sense of peace came from.

We came to a turn about three miles from my home, and suddenly I saw white feathered wings out the side and front windows of the car. I immediately thought of a bird, but it was pitch dark, and there were no white birds in this area, at least not with wings that large.

I shrugged my shoulders and drove on. A few seconds later I saw the wings again, and this time I could see a white glowing mass about a foot above the windshield. I knew deep inside that this was not a bird but an angel. I felt excited and awestruck, yet questioned myself, since my child didn't seem to see it.

Then after I had driven about another seventy-five feet it appeared to me one more time. As I slowed the car at a turn, the bright, white glowing mass hovered above the car, with wings still visible from the side windows. I never could have imagined wings so perfect, so white, and so large. They disappeared, and I drove another fifty feet. I didn't say anything to my child, who sat there quietly.

Then he calmly said, "Mom, there is a huge white bird flying over our car. It must be a giant eagle or something." I felt overjoyed at this point, knowing that what I had seen was real.

I asked my son what he had seen. He hadn't seen a bird, only big, white, glowing wings up above the car. He couldn't imagine what else it could be except a giant eagle or something.

I felt I was just keeping my head above water before this, and slowly sinking. Now I feel as though I have been given a life raft and oars. As much as I have always believed I was not alone in my struggles, I now have proof. I know there is an angel helping me through and a God who really cares.

23

IN THE PRESENCE OF ANGELS

Not all such appearances involve wings. Sometimes angels hitch a ride in other ways. When Truman E., of Seward, Nebraska, was a fairly young Christian, he read a book about angels that fascinated him. He writes:

> After reading this book, all I could think about was how great it would be to actually see an angel.
>
> I was working at the time about twenty-five miles from my hometown here in Nebraska. Those miles that I drove daily gave me time to meditate and be alone with God.
>
> This one morning, as the sun was making its appearance on the eastern horizon, I thought, *Wouldn't it be great to see an angel.* I then started to pray my daily morning prayers. I thanked God for how good He had been to me, and I mentioned that I would like to see an angel. No sooner had the words left my mouth than I looked on the right front fender of my car. There, sitting on the fender, was this huge person, even though we were going fifty-five miles per hour down the road. No, he didn't have wings, but there was no doubt in my mind that God had sent this angel to me. I know that God sends His angels to look over us here on planet Earth.

Most of the stories in this book do not involve wings. But here is one more that does.

Beverly M., of Dickinson Center, New York, had to go up to St. Regis Falls on an errand one night. Coming home, she felt impressed to stop at a woman's house. Beverly rang the bell a couple of times before the woman came to the door. The two had a very good visit together. The woman had somehow drifted out of the church. They talked of many things; Beverly especially mentioned the ministry of angels, of the many narrow escapes she had had, and how she felt strongly that God had sent angels to protect and keep her from harm and danger. In fact, for the past few weeks, she had been driving a car with faulty brakes, but before she left the house, she prayed for God to protect her.

It is important to point out here that we should never be presumptuous and expect God to protect us from our own laziness or folly. But sometimes He does anyway. Perhaps it was because Beverly was on a mission of mercy that God protected her.

Before she left, she asked the woman if they might pray together. The woman said, "Oh yes, please do!" They knelt together, and Beverly prayed.

As the woman looked up, tears were streaming down her face. She said, "Beverly, God sent you here tonight. I was so discouraged and depressed. Keep praying for me; don't give up on me."

Beverly assured her she would certainly continue to pray and told the woman she just knew she would see her come walking into church some day.

Beverly left and started for home. It was very dark, but her heart was dancing, as the heart often does after ministering to someone in need. She was singing the song, "Surely the Presence of the Lord Is in This Place." The song includes the words "I can hear the brush of angel's wings."

As she was going down a very steep hill, she suddenly heard the sound of wings flapping together. To her utter amazement, spread over the hood of her car and extending far beyond it, she saw the biggest pair of wings she had ever seen. They were pure white!

Instantly, she said right out loud, "Jesus, is that my guardian angel?"

She heard a soft whisper, "I have sent your angel to protect you." Just a few seconds later, the angel was gone, but Beverly's heart was singing all the way home!

She drove her car the rest of the week without any problems. On Saturday night, her husband, a mechanic, took the car into his garage to work on the brakes. When he started to take the wheel apart, broken pieces just fell out onto the floor!

Beverly says her experience gave new meaning to Psalm 91:4, 10: "He will cover you with his feathers, and under his wings you will find refuge. . . . No harm will befall you."

Sometimes angels appear wingless but wearing white robes, like the angel in Jesus' empty tomb, mentioned in Mark 16:5.

In October of 1991, Mrs. Leona A., of Battle Ground, Washington, was worrying over personal problems. Things bothered her so much she wasn't getting much sleep.

One night she prayed more earnestly than usual that nothing would come of a mistake she had made. "I really need Your help, Lord. I can't do it by myself. Please help me in my work."

That night, after sleeping an hour or so, she woke up at 12:30 a.m. She turned over in bed, facing the wall in her room. The room was dark. But soon she saw a beautiful white-robed being beside her bed and a hand extending down from the fold in his garment. All she could see was the lower part from the waist to the level of her bed. In astonishment she said, "Oh, Lord, thank You for being with me. I know now You will help me."

Just then, she heard two hard pounds on the side of her house. She said out loud, "What is going on outside?" Then, "Thank You, Lord, for being with me and protecting me."

Soon the being was lifted up toward the ceiling and was gone. After that, she had wonderful peace, and her problem was resolved. Leona writes, "I needed this encouragement to help me understand that God really cares for us, and He let me know in a visible way that He is always near."

Children seem to see angel wings more often than adults. Trudie H., of Wayne, Michigan, was only eight years old when she saw an angel one night after she was tucked into bed. Her room was on the top floor in a very old house. Whenever the furnace came on, it made scary creaking noises, and Trudie couldn't sleep for fear that there was something spooky under her bed.

So she did what all little girls and boys should do when they're scared—she prayed to Jesus:

> In a quick minute, an angel descended right through my ceiling onto my floor. He must have stood at least seven feet tall, with very broad shoulders and a big, strong face. He had a white robe on with a gold belt around the waist. There was a glow about him that lighted up the room. He didn't say anything to me. I just looked at him, and a peace came over me. Then I rolled over and went right to sleep.

Wings or robes, dungarees or overalls—angels always dress appropriately for the occasion. And hurting hearts seem to attract them like a magnet and cause them to dress up in their finest attire.

In 1957, Skye H. found herself lying ill in Paradise Valley Hospital in San Diego:

> I heard the family and doctor express concern over my recovery. As I prayed, as only a trusting twelve-year-old can, I was impressed to open my eyes. There, standing at the foot of my bed, was a lovely man in a white robe. He told me not to worry because Jesus had heard my prayer and was already healing me. It gave me peace, and I could not tell anyone for a long time,

because I'd been so ill I couldn't speak.

I still feel the wonderment that as Jesus rules the busy universe, He still has time to care for a twelve-year-old girl.

So why do angels sometimes appear to us with wings? Perhaps so they can give them to us. They seek to give our spirit wings so we can soar above the burdens and worries of life.

But most of the time, angels who appear to men and women look less like angels and more like refined gentlemen. How, then, can you test the suspicion that you are talking to a real angel?

If you should ever encounter someone you suspect is an angel, and you have the presence of mind to remember this, then, first, never let the angel out of your sight. That way, he won't be able to disappear behind your back.

Secondly, why not indulge in a little holy mischief! Start praising God out loud by reciting or singing the doxology:

> Praise God from whom all blessings flow.
> Praise Him all creatures here below;
> Praise Him above, ye heavenly hosts;
> Praise Father, Son, and Holy Ghost.

Watch and see what the reaction is. We have a sneaking suspicion that angels will never simply ignore the praises of God but will always join in. Protocol, you know. Or maybe they just can't help it. And who knows, maybe you'll get to hear the choir!

---

1. See also Ruth 2:12; Psalm 17:8; 36:7; 61:4; 63:7; 91:4; Matthew 23:37.

CHAPTER

3

God's Comfort Squad

Jesus is Lord.

I'm sixty-four years old. Yes, I believe in angels. Several odd things have happened to me. I'll tell you this one.

We lived upstairs in an old house that was about to fall apart. I got sick and couldn't work. Had no food. No money. No food stamps. I would never ask for help. I was ashamed. But one morning everyone was gone, and I had left the hall door open. My bed was by the door.

All of a sudden a man walked by my bed with a box of food. We had old wooden steps. No carpet on them. You could hear anyone who went up and down the steps. But I heard no one this time. The man walked by me. Didn't speak or even look at me. He set the box on the table and was walking out. Still he didn't speak or look at me. He was in the doorway.

I said ,"Thank you. Who are you?"

He then turned his head to me and smiled and said, "I am an angel of the Lord." I jumped out of bed. He was gone in a flash. No one went down the stairs. And no door to the outside opened. I was in the hallway. It shook me up at first. Like lightning, he was gone, and I got over my sickness. Praise God. Isn't Jesus wonderful?

—Rufus M., Indianapolis, Indiana.

In the summer of 1987, my husband, myself, and four small children (ages one to five), drove from Oregon to Arkansas to visit my mother. We took all our money (which wasn't much— my husband is on SSI disability) for that month and left for this trip.

After four days of driving, we parked in the middle of the night in a parking lot area in Oklahoma City, about a block from a mini-market. My husband was tired, so the children and I sat outside the car on a blanket while he rested. The children were restless and hungry. I dug into my pockets and found enough money for a small package of doughnuts for them. I walked to the store quickly while the children rested, praying God would watch over them.

After I came back, I sat down and turned around to see a man standing over us. I should have been scared, but I had peace. He asked if he could get the children some milk, so I said OK. I didn't see him go into the store, because the baby was crying. In a few minutes, he was back. In the sack he gave us, I found milk, cups, and a large package of doughnuts for us. The baby was crying more, so I looked down to comfort him. When I looked up to thank the man, he was nowhere in sight. There was nowhere for him to go, since it was an open parking lot. I thank Jesus for watching over us.

—Mrs. Steve R., Jefferson, Oregon.

We serve a tender-hearted God, who is "the Father of compassion and the God of all comfort, who comforts us in all our troubles" (2 Corinthians 1:3, 4). Notice Isaiah's gentle portrait of this divine Comforter:

Comfort, comfort my people, says your God.

Shout for joy, O heavens; rejoice, O earth; burst into song, O mountains! For the Lord comforts his people and will have compassion on his afflicted ones.

I, even I, am he who comforts you. Who are you that you fear mortal men, the sons of men, who are but grass?

In all their distress he too was distressed, and the angel of his presence saved them. In his love and mercy he redeemed them; he lifted them up and carried them all the days of old.

As a mother comforts her child, so will I comfort you; and you will be comforted over Jerusalem (Isaiah 40:1; 49:13; 51:1; 63:9; 66:13).

IN THE PRESENCE OF ANGELS

Whenever possible, God uses human beings to bring comfort to others, as in the case of Paul and Titus ("God, who comforts the downcast, comforted us by the coming of Titus" [2 Corinthians 7:6]). But sometimes, when He's fresh out of corporeal comforters, He uses angels.

At first thought, sending angels to provide mere comfort may seem to violate God's usual economy of miracles. We can understand God using an angel to save a life or accomplish something tangible; but just to make a child of God feel better? Just to alleviate anxiety? Why should God waste time relieving someone's worry about something that may never come to pass anyway?

But He does. The most common sentence uttered by angels to human beings is, "Don't be afraid."

J. S. B., from Zapata, Texas, is a schoolteacher who had been fighting severe depression for four years. His constant worrying was producing physical symptoms such as hair loss. Then he came to know God and accepted Jesus as his personal Saviour.

One night he was sound asleep, when he suddenly heard music. It sounded like harps playing. He writes:

> I woke up and looked in all directions. Suddenly, beside my bed was a huge being of peace with wavy hair, dressed in a peach-colored garment. It said to me, "Don't worry anymore." I felt a warmth and peaceful feeling. He then quickly disappeared.

When Paul's future looked stormy, God sent an angel: "Last night an angel of the God whose I am and whom I serve stood beside me and said, 'Do not be afraid, Paul. You must stand trial before Caesar; and God has graciously given you the lives of all who sail with you' " (Acts 27:23, 24).

When Zechariah was discouraged by the difficulties his people encountered in rebuilding Jerusalem, God communicated comfort to him through his angel: "So the Lord spoke kind and comforting words to the angel who talked with me.... This is what the Lord Almighty says: 'My towns will again overflow with prosperity, and the Lord will again comfort Zion and choose Jerusalem' " (Zechariah 1:13, 17).

God sent angels to comfort Jesus at the end of His forty-day fast in the desert (see Matthew 4:11) and at the end of His struggle in the Garden of Gethsemane (see Luke 22:43).

Sometimes God sends food, as He did for Rufus M. and Mrs. R., not to prevent starvation, but just for comfort. When Elijah was tired and discouraged after fleeing from wicked Queen Jezebel, God sent an angelic chef to cook him two meals (see 1 Kings 19:5-8), and this "heaven-cooked meal" kept him going for forty days without further nourishment!

Evidently, God cares about our feelings. He understands the corrosive effect of continual anxiety on the human psyche. So sometimes He sends an angel. . . .

I walked along that morning with a heavy heart. I was on my way to the hospital. Today, I was scheduled to take a blood transfusion. I was seriously anemic, and this was the only way I would be able to give birth to the child I was expecting.

I had been a believer for about four years. We had a very divided house. I was struggling to rear our four older children in the fear of the Lord, with only the ridicule of an unbelieving spouse instead of support.

I was about to step up onto the sidewalk leading to the bus stop, when an older woman joined me. After exchanging greetings, the woman said, "I know that things do not look too good right now, but hold on. God will see you through."

I felt my burden being lifted. My joy was returning. My faith was being restored! The bus was coming to our stop. I waited until the woman boarded the bus and then stepped on after her.

3—I.P.A.

I paid my fare and looked for the precious woman to say thanks. She was nowhere on the bus!

I found my seat and strangely felt no surprise. I was able to recall the story in Genesis, chapter 18, verses 1 to 9, where the three men visited Abraham in the Plains of Mamre in the heat of the day. It was revealed later that these were indeed angels. "Are they not all ministering spirits, sent forth to minister for them who shall be heirs of salvation?" (Hebrews 1:14, KJV).

I was much encouraged by that messenger that morning. I am still on the battlefield for the Lord. Forty-two years in traveling, and I am not tired yet.

—Wanda T., Houston, Texas.

This event took place ten years ago in January of 1981. A few weeks after accepting the Lord Jesus as my Saviour, I went alone to keep an appointment to look at an apartment in an unfamiliar section of our city. I uttered a desperate prayer asking the Lord to aid me in finding the apartment complex.

When I arrived at the site, I wandered about, trying to find the manager's office. I asked several people, but no one seemed to know where the office was.

Suddenly, a very nice, clean-cut, neatly dressed young man appeared and offered to show me to the manager's office. He had a soft, peaceful manner and a glow about his face. As we walked along, I told him of my need to find an apartment. I also told him that I was planning to attend the Friday-evening service at my church after the appointment. He assured me that everything would be all right.

It was very dark, and I knew I was fortunate to have his protection. When we arrived at the office, I went down two stairs toward the basement and then decided to go back to thank the nice young man who had helped me. I turned around and went back, but he was gone.

There were several people standing just outside the door. When I asked if they'd seen the young man, they looked at me as if I was crazy and told me that I had walked over to the office alone. I ran around looking for him but never did find the beautiful young man whom I believe was an angel.

The Lord takes very good care of us, doesn't He?

—Sharon G., North Tonawnada, New York.

I grew up in my grandmother's home because my father had died. My grandmother was a godly woman, so I grew up knowing that angels encamped around me. However, the first time one manifested his presence was in 1942 or 1943.

It happened in East Liverpool, Ohio. I was very young, and my baby son was about eighteen months old. My husband had just left (by choice) for the navy with little warning to me. That night, I was left alone to close the house before walking to the corner to catch a bus that would take me to live with my in-laws. I was feeling very alone and a little frightened. I went to the basement to make certain everything was securely locked. As I got to the stairway to come up, standing there was a lovely, tall, white shining being. I then knew I was not alone, and that experience sustained me through a trying time in the days ahead.

In 1952 I was again alone with my son and my little daughter, who was just about three years old at the time. My husband had left us and was remarried. We lived in California. I had taken my daughter with me to do some laundry, and as I backed out to leave the parking lot, the door of the car on her side flew open, and my daughter fell under my car.

After taking her to the doctor and coming back home again, I was sitting alone in the living room and praying. Suddenly, in the corner of the room by the front window, the same wonderful being appeared. The same peaceful assurance came, and I knew my daughter would be fine.

Time passed, and life moved on, but not always as I would have wanted.

In 1980, I was living in Durham, Massachusetts. I was working as a waitress in a nearby town. It was Thanksgiving Day, and I had just gotten off work. It was raining—just pouring—as I started toward home. I could hardly see the road. I passed through a little town on the way, and as I was rounding a bend, my car began to slide. I could see I was heading straight for a large pole. I called out loud, "Dear Jesus!" Suddenly, my car was stopped, seemingly by an unseen force, only inches from the pole. Standing there was that same lovely white shining being—and again, I was filled with peace and calmness.

—Georgetta W., Redlands, California.

Some years back I was in the hospital, and my daughter was at home. Her daddy was working the night shift, so she was home alone. I asked the Lord to show me that He would protect her so that I could get some rest. I fell asleep and had a very short dream.

During that dream, I saw my front yard. Up by the driveway, I saw a beautiful, shining angel with a gold sword in his hand. At another corner, over near a large pecan tree, I saw another angel. I immediately knew that the Lord heard and answered my prayers. I can never stop thanking Him for sending those two

guardian angels to watch over my daughter.
—Jean S., Morris, Alabama.

I married young, and my first husband was an alcoholic. I gave birth to my first child when I was only five-and-one-half months pregnant.

Colette was two pounds and three ounces, and life had been disappointing until Colette. She was the one good thing in my life and became my whole world.

She was home a month, and had gotten up to seven pounds, when she died suddenly of what they called crib death. With no one to turn to, I began to pray. I asked God, "Are You there? Is my baby suffering? How could it be fair to punish an innocent child?" I just couldn't cope. I needed help; I felt like I was dying.

My prayers were interrupted with an unexplained feeling, and immediately I thought of a prowler, which frightened me.

For several nights, the same thing happened, and then it dawned on me: Every time I prayed I had this feeling. I wondered, "God, could that be You? If it is, could You help me not to be frightened?"

A peace came over me, and I was impressed to sit up. That idea frightened me too. I sat there, and then I opened my eyes and an angel appeared.

The angel really changed the direction of my thoughts. This child was not mine but God's child. She was a gift from God even for that short time. I was comforted to learn that there really was a God.

I believe my angel was allowed to visit me, not because I'm anyone special, because we're all special to God, but for the simple reason that I had no one else, and God knew it.

IN THE PRESENCE OF ANGELS

I learned that God doesn't cause suffering but rather suffers right along with us.

–Marilynn S.

Sometimes God sends angels to comfort us even when we don't deserve it.

Jacob was a scheming scoundrel. He stole the birthright from his brother Esau and then fled for his life. The story is told in Genesis chapters 25 to 27.

On the second night of this journey, tired and alone, Jacob lay down on the open ground to sleep, discouraged and depressed. He knew that if he returned home, Esau would kill him. If he fled to a distant country, he might never see his kinfolk again. Would he be able to find work? Would he make friends? Would his brother come looking for him? Would he ever enjoy life again?

Laboring under a sense of guilt, perhaps he thought, *After what I've done, God has surely turned His back on me. I can't expect any help from Him.* Nevertheless, Jacob must have confessed his sins and asked God to forgive him. Then he fell asleep. And dreamed.

In his dream he saw a stairway reaching from earth to heaven, perhaps like the stairs up the side of an ancient Near-Eastern ziggurat, or stepped pyramid. On these stairs, angels of God were ascending and descending (see Genesis 28:12).

God was standing at the top of this stairway, speaking words of comfort and hope. He assured Jacob that He would give his descendants the land he was lying on. Then He said, "I am with you and will watch over you wherever you go, and I will bring you back to this land. I will not leave you until I have done what I have promised you" (verse 15).

Many centuries later, Jesus said to some of His disciples: "I tell you the truth, you shall see heaven open, and the angels of God ascending and descending on the Son of Man" (John 1:51).

Jacob's vision was a mini-parable of the gospel. How is Jesus like a stairway? He and His angels are the basic link between earth and heaven.

Encouraged by the dream, Jacob continued his journey with a deep sense of God's presence and the watch care of heavenly angels.

Twenty years later, God told him to return home to Canaan. Now he had a large family and many flocks and herds. As far as he knew, his brother still wanted to kill him. The news of Jacob and his slow-moving entourage would certainly go ahead of him. So there was the real possibility Esau might try to ambush him somewhere along the way. But Jacob continued on his way, trusting God.

At one point, God showed Jacob an army of angels guarding him (see Genesis 32:1). But Jacob saw these angels only briefly. The rest of the time, they were invisible. A visible angel is the exception, not the rule. Nevertheless, they are always near us, ready to protect, comfort, and lift us out of gloom and despondence.

It was about four years ago. I had heart trouble and was about to have bypass surgery. I had some overnight guests from out of town, so I let them have my bed while I took the couch. It was a narrow couch. I tried to avoid sleeping on my left side, but I must have turned over in my sleep, because the next thing I knew, someone was waking me up. I realized I was numb. When this person got me turned over, I got a glimpse of a shining angel with a golden glow. I said, "My mouth is so dry."

She said, "I know," and vanished. Then I noticed my mouth was moist.

IN THE PRESENCE OF ANGELS

The next day I pondered this wondrous thing, for I didn't think I was worthy of a guardian angel.

I also had another, even greater experience forty years ago. At that time, I had a little two-and-a-half-year-old daughter who became sick and experienced brain damage. Any sudden noise would cause her to jerk and fall over. It became so bad that she once knocked out some teeth. She was always getting hurt.

I took her to different doctors, but they were unable to help. I was thinking about taking her in my arms and stepping out in front of a truck or something to end it all.

One Sunday afternoon I was listening to the radio church program as I sat by my window. I started praying and looking up at the sky. I said, "Dear Lord, please forgive me," and I named every sin I could think of. Then I said, "But I guess I can't go to heaven because I have been divorced and remarried." At that moment, I saw this figure slowly come down from the sky. He was in the form of a shepherd with wings. I saw a staff in his hand. He landed in our garden a few yards away. He became like a white, bright cloud with wings. I saw his smiling mouth, his nose, but for some reason, not his eyes. It became very quiet around me.

I was changed that day. I started to read the Bible, and when I read where Jesus said, "I am the Good Shepherd," that phrase seemed to jump out of the page. I didn't take all this lightly. It was awesome!

My child never got completely well, but I was able to bear it somehow.

—Cornelia T., Hurricane, West Virginia.

Some months ago, when I knew my daughter must die, I prayed God to take me first, as I felt I could not endure her death.

I felt I'd die beside her or lose my mind in unbearable grief. I wept; I prayed to die first.

But it was not to be. Still, I could not go to the funeral. So I arranged to view her privately and alone. As I entered the chapel and the door closed, I stood there. I could not take a step. I saw her up front, but I could not go. I prayed, Lord Jesus, walk with me, or I cannot go to her. My feet were rooted to the floor.

Instantly, a strong presence came to my side, so powerful I could feel it, and I almost saw someone. This strong presence took my arm, and a voice said, "Come, I'll go with you." I looked to see who, but saw no one. I felt only a presence.

My feet began to walk; I walked boldly and well to the casket. I am very feeble and can barely walk, but I walked that day. I felt strong and well, and I was strengthened to gaze on my darling's lovely face. I sat by her side sorrowfully, but not overcome, not devastated, not hysterical. The marvelous presence stood beside me. I remembered Christ in the garden. An angel came and strengthened Him. Thus it was with me. I touched her cold hands, kissed her cold face, and felt it a privilege to be there, saying, 'Goodbye, I'll meet you in our Father's house.'

—Nita Marie Law[1]

How well I remember the day back in 1958 when I found the lump in my son Tommie's leg. He was two-and-a-half years old at the time. Our new baby boy, Robert, was six weeks old. Daughter Joan was twelve, and son Jackson was ten. The strength of my husband kept me stable.

We took Tommie to the doctor, and he recommended applying hot salt packs for three days, which we did. Nothing changed. So Tommie went to the hospital, where a biopsy revealed that it

41

was (that awful word) "malignant." I remember Rose A. helping me get my courage up to call the doctor to find out the results.

From that day on, life began to fall apart. Tommie had a first operation in February, a second in June, followed by two weeks of radiation treatments that left his leg looking like he had a bad sunburn. It was a terrible summer!

By October he was having abdominal pain, and we had to take him back to the hospital for the third time. There wasn't much more that could be done except to try to keep him comfortable with medications. I recall saying to the doctor, "I'm going to have faith."

At this time I knew a lot of people were praying. I was at my lowest ebb when Mr. and Mrs. Holland came to visit me. She said to me, "Be still, and know that I am God." It was at this point that Jesus came into focus. I'd been trying desperately to find Him.

Then something happened that first week of October.

One evening I wheeled Tommie to the exit door, hoping and praying to meet a nurse or someone to take him back to his room. It was wrenching pain to leave him at 8:00 p.m. I met a woman that evening near the exit. We exchanged a few words, and she told me she had a twelve-year-old son in the children's ward and also a husband upstairs, and she could stay later. They had been injured in a automobile accident.

This woman was a complete stranger to me, but in the very first moments I talked to her, I liked her. And she said to me, "I'll take him." I was overwhelmed (and still am to this day), as she was there to meet us every night for the next two-and-a-half months until Tommie couldn't be put in the wheelchair anymore. A week later, on December 22, he died. She had never missed a night! I know beyond a shadow of a doubt that it was Jesus visiting me. She was my "angel"!

I've suffered, but I've been healed. I have despaired but have recovered hope. Before this happened, I knew the Twenty-third Psalm; now I know the Shepherd.

—Mrs. Alice T., Durham, Maine.

In the time-honored custom of saving the best for last, we bring you a story that might be entitled "A Visit From Gabriel." It's one of the most important angel stories in this book because of the significance of the messenger and his message.

In all of the biblical accounts of angel appearances, only once does an angel introduce himself by name. It happens in Luke 1:19. An angel appears to Zechariah, father of John the Baptist, and says, "I am Gabriel. I stand in the presence of God, and I have been sent to speak to you and to tell you this good news." This is the same angel who had appeared to Daniel more than five hundred years earlier. Shortly after talking to Zechariah, he brought a message to Mary, the mother of Jesus.

That is the last we hear of Gabriel in the Bible. Would you like to know what Gabriel has been up to lately? Well, he appeared to Vincent T. in 1993, and I think you'll be fascinated by what he had to say.

Juanita Kretschmar, a trustworthy friend, called Vincent and heard from his own lips the account of what happened in the wee hours of the morning of March 26, 1993. We are indebted to her for this account.

Vincent is an analytical chemist at a private laboratory in Chattanooga. One day Vincent's sister called from Singapore to say that his mom had complications related to a heart condition. For the next week, Vincent worried about her.

About a week later, on a Thursday night, he was working late to complete certain tests whose results were due on Friday. During the evening, he had moved his new car close to the front door of the building, since there had been criminal activity in the area not too long before. From time to time, he looked out the window, into the almost-empty parking lot, to make sure his new car had not been stolen.

IN THE PRESENCE OF ANGELS

At 1:30 a.m. he finally finished working in the lab. As he was preparing to lock the door, he saw a person standing by the passenger side of his car. He assumed the man was trying to steal it and was perhaps working with a companion, who was no doubt already in the car on the driver's side.

Unsure what to do, Vincent went into the lab and prayed silently, "Lord, help me to do what I have to do. Do I have to use chi-sao?" (Chi-sao was the most effective form of martial arts for that situation.) He looked around the lab and selected an eighteen-inch metal rod used to pick up samples in the laboratory testing procedures. Keeping the rod behind him, he decided to leave by another door, one closer to where his car was parked. Still praying for help and wanting to be a Christian, Vincent stuck his head out that door and called out to the stranger beside his car, "Hi! Can I help you?"

The stranger spoke to him. "Hi, Vincent."

Vincent was startled and asked, "Do I know you?"

The stranger said, "Not really."

"What is your name? Who are you?" Vincent probed, still trying to see where the other companions to the stranger were lurking.

The stranger answered, "I have the name of your primary and secondary school." Then he added, "I'm a friend. You don't have to use the chi-sao or the rod on me."

Now Vincent was really startled. No one he knew, not even his best friend in this country, was familiar with the form of martial arts referred to as chi-sao. Nor did anyone, to his knowledge, know he knew it.

Vincent asked the man, "How do you know that?"

The stranger answered, "I know. By the way, your mom is fine." Then the stranger said to Vincent, "You love the Lord very much, don't you?"

Vincent said, "That's right."

The stranger said, "He loves you very much too." Then he added, "He's coming very, very soon."

Vincent answered, "That's great."

The stranger asked, "Can I have a cup of water?"

Vincent said, "Sure," and he turned momentarily to get him the water. Then he decided to invite the stranger inside to drink from the water fountain. He was still afraid this water errand was just a trap to give whoever was out there a chance to drive off in the car. Vincent turned back to invite the man inside, but the stranger had vanished. Vincent hadn't had his head turned more than three seconds. There was no place for the man to have gone.

Not wanting to go all the way back into the laboratory, Vincent lay the rod down by the front door and headed home—puzzled. When he came back to work later that morning, he wondered if he had dreamed the whole experience. As a scientist, he wanted proof that it had really happened.

When he got to the building, he found the rod lying by the door. He knew for sure he had not been dreaming. The first thing he did when he entered the laboratory was to lock himself in the restroom and kneel in prayer. Vincent asked God, "Show me what I have to do, Lord. I know what I remember. If I'm supposed to share it, I must believe it myself."

With a sense of awe, he sat at his computer and wrote out in detail the entire experience. That evening, he finally told a friend about it. The friend immediately asked what primary and secondary school he had attended. Vincent told him that although he had been raised a Buddhist, his parents sent him to a Catholic primary and secondary school. The name was St. Gabriel.

That night, Vincent continued to ask God what He wanted with the experience. As he slept, he relived the entire experience in a dream, seeing himself and hearing word for word the entire conversation. He wanted accuracy, and going through the experience in a dream verified that.

You might be interested to know how Vincent became a Christian. He found the offer for a "Voice of Prophecy" Bible course stuck in the pages of a book about nuclear physics he was reading in a library in Singapore years ago. The title of the book began with the word *Transformation.* A year after he received his first Bible lesson, he was baptized. Today, this Chinese man is a devout Seventh-day Adventist Christian.

Juanita asked Vincent about his personal walk with the Lord. He said he believes we need to be ready to meet Jesus every moment of every day. He said he feels it is important to spend the very first moment of every day with God, and he has studied his own schedule and has chosen to tithe one-tenth of his productive time. So he gives the first hour and a half each day to his Lord. As he put it, "We need to set priorities."

Then Vincent revealed something that probably explains why he had this unique experience. For some time prior to his encounter with Gabriel, he had been asking God, "Am I ready to meet Jesus right now?"

Isn't it wonderful that God loves Vincent so much he would send Gabriel to reassure him of his love! Come to think of it—now, this is very exciting—there is a pattern here, because in two of his four biblical appearances, Gabriel did the very same thing he did for Vincent. In Daniel 9:23 Gabriel told Daniel, "You are highly esteemed." And in Luke 1:28 Gabriel said to Mary, "Greetings, you who are highly favored! The Lord is with you." And in 1993, Gabriel told Vincent, "God loves you very much." Evidently, it is a high honor to be visited by this angel.

Now, friend, the question is, are YOU ready to meet Jesus right now? Don't expect a visit from Gabriel. Christ may come before that. Gabriel said, "He's coming very, very soon." If He came tomorrow—or today—would you be ready to meet Him? Think about it.

---

1. Letter to *Adventist Review,* 18 February 1988, 4.

4

The Great Physician and His Hospital Helpers

A shiver of fear passed through my body as I entered the huge medical facility. It reminded me of the medical offices where my husband and I had spent so many hours waiting for blood transfusions for him only two years ago—or was it two centuries ago? Since then, I had borne the agonizing burden of being alone, without someone to discuss problems and help me make decisions; and with all the responsibility of providing for the children's daily needs. And now this. Would the doctor diagnose my problem as cancer also? Would our four

47

young children have to spend the rest of their lives without a mother as well as a father?

As I walked down the long hall, with worry my closest companion, my thoughts were interrupted when I saw the name "Dr. Everhart" (the doctor with whom I had my appointment) on the office door. Just as I stepped inside the office, I noticed a doctor heading in my direction. I was startled. How familiar he looked! He also appeared surprised when he saw me.

"Hello, there," he exclaimed. "How are you?"

I had an almost overwhelming desire to stop right on the spot and tell him how I really was, but instead, I paused for a second, said, "Hi! Oh, I'm OK, I guess," and then walked on to the reception desk.

The nurse greeted me, took my medical history, showed me to the examining room, and gave me a gown. "Dr. Everhart should be here in a few minutes," she said. I lay down on the table staring at the sterile ceiling, wondering if the man in the white jacket I had said "Hi" to was Dr. Everhart. I was imagining what he might have said if I had poured out my troubles, loneliness, and fear to him, when the door opened quietly, and the same doctor crossed the room and stood beside me. His warm, broad hand covered mine.

"When I saw you in the waiting room, I sensed that you were frightened," he remarked. "Do you want to tell me about it?" I had never heard a kinder voice.

Without any hesitation, the frustrations and anxieties of these two years since my husband's death poured from my mouth like steam from a locomotive.

When I paused long enough to get my breath, he interjected, "You must know by now, I'm not here to examine you but rather to let you know I care." Then he cautioned, when I finally finished talking, "Don't be afraid of life. This period will pass, and you'll have plenty of sunny days ahead. But do try to break the pattern of worry." Remind yourself that very few things people worry about ever materialize."

With a twinkle in his eye, as though he knew some special secret, he promised, "I'll see you sometime again," and then closed the door.

When Dr. Everhart finally came in and started the much-dreaded examination, I realized I truly had worried needlessly. When he said, "Good news! You have nothing wrong that good medicine won't cure," I knew the bend in the road was straightening.

I fairly floated the fifteen miles home from San Jose that day, not so much because of the doctor's good report but because someone had listened to me and cared.

I noticed my neighbor Marvis working in her garden as I pulled into my driveway, so I ran across the street to talk to her. She had made my appointment with Dr. Everhart because, as a nurse, she knew all the "best doctors" in the city.

"Marvis, I've just come from the doctor's office. Thank you so much for making the arrangements. He really knew what he was doing—I was impressed with his ability—and he told me I was going to be just fine!" The words tumbled over each other.

"I'm so glad!" she said, smiling.

"But there's something I want to ask you, friend. All the way home I was puzzled about the first doctor I talked to in the office. He seemed so special! I've never met anyone kinder or more sympathetic, but I never did ask him his name. I'm sure you know who I mean, don't you? I kept wondering about his age too."

Marvis looked puzzled. "I sure can't help you. There is no other doctor in that office," she stated with finality. "Dr. Everhart is it. It's definitely a one-doctor office, and I've heard him say it always will be."

"Thanks anyway," I called. Now I was really puzzled.

Several days later, I saw my friend Lillian Bransby, an English-woman who fascinated me because of her intelligence and interest in life. When I told her the details of my experience in the doctor's office, she exclaimed without hesitation, "My dear, you have had an encounter with an angel. The Bible often talks about angels sent to comfort people in distress."

"But why would God, if there is a God, send an angel to me?" I asked, perplexed. "I've never done anything except run away from God." I was surprised to hear myself say that. Until that moment, I had not been conscious that I felt that way.

Lillian's expression didn't change. She didn't look either surprised or shocked but casually explained, "The Bible says they're sent to minister to people who are going to be saved."

"Saved? Saved from what? Saved for what?" I questioned, confused. Though I grew up in a church, I had never heard that word used. Saved by whom? Was there more to life than I'd known? Could this saving be an answer to that emptiness I sometimes felt? I had wondered for years what the purpose of life was and what I could do to fill the void.

"Lillian, I've heard about the exciting Bible class you teach. Do you suppose it would be all right if I started coming? Do you think you could help me?"

The wrinkles crinkled around her eyes as she laughed in reply.

"Yes to the last question. It definitely might help. We'll look for you next Tuesday morning at the bank meeting room at ten o'clock."

"OK, I'll be there," I promised as I waved goodbye and continued on home.

That was the beginning of the greatest change in my life. Faithfully, for four years, I went to Lillian's Bible study. I became more excited each week. I learned who God is, who I am, and what Jesus Christ has done for me. I finally understood personally what the word *saved* meant. The Bible explained clearly why there is so much trouble in the world, so even the newspapers make sense now.

My life began to bear evidence that "old things pass away, all things became new" (2 Corinthians 5:17) through Jesus Christ. I often remember, with delight, my experience in the doctor's office. I recall the extraordinary flow of love and concern from the angel God sent that day. I thank God again and again for caring for me even when I didn't know Him or care about Him; for sending comfort to me when I needed it most; for starting me on the special path that gave meaning to my life!

—Martha G., East Wenatchee, Washington.

If there is one type of person whom angels impersonate more than any other, with the possible exception of auto mechanics, it is medical professionals. Medicine can be a means of power, pride, and wealth, or it can be a ministry. Jesus considers all selfless ministry to the sick as if done to Himself, for He said to His followers, "I was sick and you looked after me" (Matthew 25:36). Sometimes, in rare cases, Jesus reverses the equation and Himself shows up to visit the sick, or He sends an angel.

When Virgil F.'s granddaughter Kathy was three years old, she was hit by a car in front of her home. She had a compound fracture in her right leg. The bones were exposed. The tire took all the skin off her foot, exposing the tendons.

While she was waiting to go into surgery, a man in a white jacket appeared at the head of her cart. He rubbed her forehead and told her she would be OK. He looked very much like the traditional picture of Christ; he had long hair, a long beard, and sandals.

When Kathy was in surgery, he brought her a little rag doll. Virgil's wife asked him if he had any children. He said No. All of a sudden, he was gone. The nurses were going in every direction in that room, so Virgil asked them who the man was, but no one else had seen him.

IN THE PRESENCE OF ANGELS

Kathy still has that rag doll today. She had a remarkable recovery—no scars, no complications. She is now in her third year at West Point Military Academy, and her leg and foot work perfectly.

Kathy is only one of many who have been ministered to in the hospital by vanishing comforters. Here are more testimonies from patients who have enjoyed the loving care of some very special doctors and nurses who weren't on the hospital payroll.

In our family there have been two occurrences in which two distinct angels in the form of nurses have appeared and ministered first to my mother Celina, who was badly burned in 1971 and was in the trauma unit, and then to my baby daughter Melody, who was dying with spinal meningitis in 1973.

In the first instance, my mother remembers seeing two nurses in her hospital room (only at night) who were constantly at her side, giving her liquids and comforting her during her agony (she had been so badly burned that not even her family was allowed in the room for fear of contamination). This occurred for several nights. When her fever broke, she was able to ask the day nurses, "Who were the nurses who cared for me at night?" The day nurses stated that there were no night nurses caring for her, or for anyone else, for that matter, since they were short-handed and were unable to give special care to anyone.

When my infant daughter became ill with spinal meningitis, she was hospitalized in the same hospital. She remained there a total of fifteen days. During this time, we didn't know whether she would live or die. In fact, the doctor stated that only a miracle would pull her out.

One day while my mother was staying with Melody, two nurses walked in and asked if they might pray for Melody's recovery. My mother was aware that she recognized these women but said nothing. After they prayed together, the two women thanked my mom and left the room. My mother went after them into the hallway to talk with them, but to her dismay, they were nowhere to be found.

My daughter's condition changed as of that day. Today, she's eighteen years old and has not one sign of her bout with meningitis.

—Theresa A., Santa Fe, New Mexico.

On March 8, 1990, I had my first mammogram. A few days later, a nurse from the doctor's office called me with the results. She said the mammogram showed a lump and I would need to find a surgeon as soon as possible. I was shocked by her words and became depressed, thinking I was surely going to die. All I could think of was CANCER. I called my family, who helped ease some of my fears, but I still felt so all alone.

After a while, I collected my thoughts and remembered seeing an ad on TV about Hutzel Hospital specializing in women's medicine. I called and was referred to a Dr. Rosenberg—he was supposed to be the best. I made an appointment with him. When I arrived, he did a breast exam and sent me upstairs for an ultrasound.

The next day, Dr. Rosenberg called, telling me I needed to set up a surgery date with his office. Things were happening too fast. I still couldn't believe it. I was really scared. I had no husband to care for my three children in case I died.

Suddenly, as that thought left, a feeling of peace swept over me. It was as if God was telling me everything would be fine.

The day of the surgery arrived. I prayed as I was being prepped for surgery.

After the operation, I was taken to a recovery room. I was asleep until someone touched my big toe and lightly squeezed it. I awakened and saw a white figure standing at the foot of my cot. He said the lump was benign and that everything was going to be all right. I fell back asleep until I was awakened by a nurse. I looked up, smiled at her, and said, "Isn't it wonderful the lump was found to be benign?"

"How would you know?" she said. I told her that the doctor had come by and told me.

"That's impossible," she said. "After your surgery, he went to another patient." I was really confused then.

Nine days later I went back to Dr. Rosenberg to have the stitches removed. "Well, Yvonne," he said, "your test results were negative." I told him that I already knew that. He had told me in the recovery room the day of the surgery. He looked bewildered and said he hadn't been to see me after surgery; I must be mistaken. I now knew for sure that it was my special guardian angel watching over me.

—Yvonne M., Westland, Michigan.

On October 22, 1966, Debra M., of Lincoln, Nebraska, ignored her premonition to stay away from the stables and went horseback riding, bareback. A stray bullet grazed the horse's back, barely missing Debra. The frightened horse bolted and ran alongside a barn, carrying Debra into the rusty blades of an old mowing sickle. When she arrived at the hospital, she required surgery for the deep lacerations that had severed the nerves and muscles of one of her legs. The doctors considered amputation, but a second surgery succeeded in reattaching the nerves, marking the beginning of long months of therapy. Finally, a third surgery in 1968 restored most of the function in the leg. Here is Debra's account of her encounter with an angel:

I was thoroughly frightened, but outwardly brave, while checking into Omaha Methodist Hospital for the third surgery. Praying for divine protection, I asked the Lord to be especially near.

While Mom and Sis helped with the unpacking, a young, tall, handsome blond man entered the room, greeted me by my full name, and introduced himself as John. He said he was expecting me.

Wow, I thought, a super-cute intern has been assigned to my case. How lucky can a girl get? (Since John was dressed in white, we assumed he was an intern, though he never said he was.)

"Seeing you have company, I'll come back when you are alone so we can talk," John said politely. I could not wait for Mom and Sis to leave. I practically pushed them from the room.

When John returned, he said he knew how frightened I was and reminded me that Jesus is ever near and that Jesus had protected me through the accident, the surgeries, everything. He even mentioned thoughts that I had never told anyone. How did John know so much about me?

John stayed constantly within close range throughout my hospital stay, giving constant support, encouragement, and help, talking about Jesus and His love.

On Saturday John stayed about fifteen hours. That afternoon, I was miserable, in pain, and mad at the world. John read while I painted. The television showed a car race. Since neither of us was watching, John asked if he could turn the set off.

"No", I snapped, slopping paint on the canvas and generally making a mess. John sat near the bed and talked soothingly. He said he knew how I was feeling.

"Debra, no matter how you feel, you must always try to do your best. Now dry your eyes, take a deep breath, and try again on the painting."

I did as instructed, and later John came over and helped

correct the mistakes. We talked for hours after that—until 10:45 p.m., to be exact. Strangely, none of the nurses chased him out; in fact, they did not even seem to know he was there!

The next morning, the hospital gave their official release. Wanting to say goodbye to John and to thank him, I asked the head nurse and a doctor where the young, tall, and handsome John was.

"John?" they queried. "No one by that name, with that description, works in this hospital in any capacity!"

I left in a daze. Was John a wonderful mirage, a figment of my imagination? No—how could other members of my family see and talk to a figment? And a mirage could not be so utterly perfect and kind and help me with my troubles.

Then the pieces fit. This was the culmination, the answer to my prayer uttered back in October 1966 for the Lord to save me from a fatal accident and to show His love and watch care over me. The Lord did care about me! The Lord had sent an angel to be with me personally, visibly, to show that He did care personally for me, for every one of us, no matter who we are.

Would I go through all this again? Yes, for I have learned so much about God and His love. I have heard a saying: God never leads us except in the way that we would choose to be led if we knew the end from the beginning.

Throughout all the pain, the suffering, the rejection from school friends, I felt very close to God and learned to trust and love Him more. In that one accident, God saved me from death many times over.

The leg is still bothersome, but I believe this keeps me humble and reminds me whom I am dependent on.

This next story happened at Saint Helena Hospital and Health Center in 1988. The facts in this story have been confirmed by Dr. Harold James and Duane Gimstadt, head chaplain of the institution. The "angel" in this story is Lloyd Funkhouser, chaplain at St. Helena and an eyewitness of the events.

Mary S. came into the hospital with infectious hepatitis and congestive heart failure. She seemed so far gone that the order was given for no "code," no life support, no hope. Mary was in Intensive Care just waiting to die.

Mary and her husband Lloyd had had a hard life with much heartache. They knew each other as children and married and lived as sharecroppers in the cotton fields of South Carolina. They had no children or living relatives.

Here is Lloyd Funkhouser's account of what happened.

When I arrived to see Mary in ICU, her husband was sitting by the bed, holding Mary's hand and sobbing. I rolled up beside him, put my arm around his shoulders, told him that I was the chaplain, and assured him that I would stay with him. He voiced his appreciation, and we wept together.

"Lloyd, are you a Christian?" I asked.

"No. We have never had any use for religion or wanted anything to do with it!" Lloyd said emphatically.

"I'd like to pray for Mary," I offered.

Lloyd replied with resignation in his voice, "We have never believed in prayer, but go ahead if you want." So I prayed as Mary continued to hang on as if "by a thread."

Two hours passed with no change. I took Lloyd to the waiting room, gave him a pillow, covered him with a blanket, and he quickly went to sleep. I returned to Mary and was praying when she quit breathing. Her eyes rolled back and were gently closed by her special nurse, Leida Jurado. The two lines on the monitor were straight and flat. Mary was dead.

I awakened Lloyd and brought him to see Mary. All they had in this world was each other, and as Lloyd stroked her hair, telling her of his love and that he could not live without her, we all wept. The nurse let down the side rail, and Lloyd took Mary up in his arms, groaning in sorrow. In a few minutes, he knelt by the bed, and with his head on her arm and holding her hand, he mourned deeply.

I pushed a chair over so Lloyd could sit beside Mary—and I prayed. "Father, I know that Your heartaches are greater than ours. Let him know that You love them, that You care and want them with You—that they are special to You!"

I was praying quietly with my arm about Lloyd when suddenly Nurse Jurado exclaimed, "She's breathing!" Sure enough, Mary *was* breathing! The straight lines on the monitor started peaking like a polygraph going wild. But too much time had passed. Mary was brain and body dead. Now she was alive but barely hanging on as before.

Again we waited two hours, but no change. Again, I put Lloyd to bed, completely exhausted. Tired myself, I had rested in the doctors' lounge for about forty-five minutes when I was paged to come quickly to ICU. I knew that Mary was dead—permanently.

I brought Lloyd into Mary's room. Praise God! Mary was alert, bright-eyed, and asking for her pulse. I had to exclaim, "Lloyd, because He loves you, God has given Mary back to you!"

It was now four o'clock, Monday morning. I visited Mary and Lloyd on the Med-Surg ward on Thursday before Mary was discharged on Friday. With beautiful smiles on both their faces, Lloyd put his arms about me and in pure joy told me, "Chaplain, I know that God loves us; I know that He answers prayer. I *believe!*"[1]

In early 1974 I was working in surgery at the Mercy Hospital in Benton Harbor, Michigan, and attending Andrews University part time.

On Tuesday, February 5, while at work, I suddenly developed a very severe headache. I lost control of my body and lost my vision. It was diagnosed as a ruptured blood vessel in my brain.

An angiogram was done on Wednesday. My physician, Dr. Kasul U., came to me after the test. He told me that the rupture was in a part of my brain that had never before been entered successfully. He told me that fourteen attempts had been made, but that all the patients had died. He said he would attempt it if I wanted, giving me a 15 percent chance of living with surgery, 0 percent without it. I asked him to go ahead and try.

Wednesday night as I lay in the ICU, I was praying—not a deathbed prayer, but just talking to God. As I prayed, the ceiling of the ICU disappeared, and I saw a wall of clouds. In the middle of the cloud, I saw a balcony. On this balcony, I saw Jesus Christ. He was looking down at me with such love and compassion. I knew everything would be OK. If I died, I would wake up in Jesus' arms. If I lived, I would serve Him.

Thursday morning, February 7, 1974, I was on the operating table in Memorial Hospital in St. Joseph, Michigan, where I had been transferred because they had better facilities for neurosurgery. Eight hours later I became the first living creature in history to survive this surgical procedure.

The next morning Dr. U. came into my room with a speech pathologist. The path through my brain that the doctor had taken was through the speech center. He suspected that I would have speech problems. He asked me, "How do you feel?"

I replied in perfect English, "Fine, but this bandage is sure tight!" They were both shocked. He said to the speech pathologist, "I guess we will not be needing you."

I was walking two days after surgery. I went home five days after surgery and was back in class in seven days.

This was not the end, though. Six weeks after surgery, I

learned that the rupture was still leaking.

Since my wife was a newly commissioned army nurse, I was transferred to Brook Army Medical Center, Fort Sam Houston, Texas. Another angiogram showed that the first diagnosis of a ruptured aneurysm was wrong. This was actually an arterial/venous malformation that required much more extensive surgery.

On May 1, 1974, I was on the operating table again. The surgeon had to remove a golf-ball-sized piece of brain tissue that contained the A/V malformation. Immediately after surgery, another angiogram was done. The leak had been stopped, but a large air bubble had developed just under the dura (tissue lining the brain). Back into surgery. An incision was made over my right temple, a small hole was drilled through my skull, and a small incision was made in the back of my head.

When I woke up, I was totally paralyzed. It took several months before I had my body back. It started with my arms, then my right leg.

I was discharged home but had to go to physical therapy three times per week. My body became stronger except for my left leg. It would not respond to any therapy.

One morning, feeling quite depressed, I fell to my knees and prayed, "Lord, please make me whole." I then got up and was doing my morning activities when suddenly I realized I was using my left leg. I fell to my knees again and thanked God.

When I got to physical therapy that day, I ran down the ramp and into the gym. All the patients suddenly stopped and looked at me. My therapist came to me and asked in astonishment, "What happened to you?!"

I just said, "I prayed."

He said, "You don't need me anymore. You have a better therapist than I will ever be!"

I now have a very slight weakness in my left leg, but no one notices. No headaches, no medication, no seizures. My EEG is normal.

I am living proof that God is still performing miracles! Many people, including my father, have accepted God because of this experience.

—Dennis C., Clayton, Wisconsin.

After Regina C., of Memphis, Tennessee, became a Christian, her grandfather told her something he had never told anyone. "Granddaddy" was a hard-working farmer who had grown up on a farm in eastern Tennessee. He couldn't read, but his spiritual life made a deep impression on Regina. "He made me want to know the Saviour he knew," she says.

In the late 1960s, he was stricken with terminal cancer and given only a few months to live. During this time of serious illness, he said, he saw angels hovering over his bed. This made a deep impression on him. He told absolutely no one at the time because he was afraid they'd think he had lost his mind.

The doctors could give no explanation when he began to improve. After he came home from the hospital, he insisted on feeding the animals and continuing his farm chores. Several years later Regina's grandfather died peacefully at home.

Samuel Guarino and Francisco Cruz, student missionaries from Mountain View College working at the Balaas Mission School in Mindanao, the Philippines, had an unusual experience while ministering to an ailing man by the name of Nardy. They were summoned to his bedside by his sister. "Nardy is feeling very sick," she said; "he wants you to come quickly. He feels he will not live long. He has a fever and has been in bed for three days without food."

Soon Samuel was on his way to the home of Nardy, guided by his sister. After an hour of hiking through thick forests, they arrived at the simple jungle hut in which Nardy lived. In the dark bamboo shelter, Samuel made out the form of Nardy wrapped in a blanket.

"Thank you for coming. Please help me," he pleaded. "Oh, my head, my head! Help me!"

Samuel placed his hand on Nardy's forehead. He was so feverish that the slightest movement sent pains through his entire body.

What should the student missionary do? He was not a doctor or a nurse. Should he give the medicine he had brought? What would happen if the man died? The entire village looked on.

Samuel prayed that God would impress him as to what to do. After prayer the idea came to him to give the sick man a sponge bath. The cooling bath made Nardy feel better. He had not slept for days, and Samuel thought fomentations would help. Using charcoal to write on a banana leaf, Samuel sent a message back to the school, where Francisco waited.

Soon Francisco arrived with fomentation cloths, and Samuel prepared to give the treatment. Before doing so they gathered the entire village for worship. To the villagers, the worship service seemed strange. Never had they attended a service to worship the God of heaven. After the closing song, Samuel offered prayer. "During that prayer we felt as though we were being lifted to heaven," Samuel said later.

Encouraged by the inspiration of the worship service, the student missionaries applied fomentations to the sick man. When the treatment ended, the patient went to sleep almost immediately.

Early the next morning, Nardy asked for something to eat. The villagers were amazed. Then an old respected man stepped forward to speak. He told the villagers that the previous afternoon he had come to the house of Nardy to offer a chicken sacrifice to bring relief to the sick man. But as he prepared to offer the sacrifice, Nardy became worse. He became so sick, in fact, that he asked the old man to discontinue the ceremony.

As the villagers listened to the story, the old man turned to face the student missionaries and said, "Your God is different from my god. I watched your actions last night, and I did not understand. When you started singing, I was sitting near the door of my hut, and I looked outside. As you began to pray for Nardy, I saw many strangers approach the house. As they came closer, I noticed they all looked handsome and were wearing white robes. Instead of walking, they appeared to float. Then I saw them surround the house just as you finished giving your treatment. Your God is different, and you are good men."

The testimony of the old man brought a change to the village. Eagerly the people listened to the message of the student missionaries. As Samuel and Francisco returned to the mission school, their hearts thrilled that God had sent His angels to help them.[2]

---

1. *Pacific Union Recorder*, 17 April 1989, 21.
2. Samuel Guarino and Francisco Cruz, as told to D. W. Christensen, "Filipino SM's Claim Angel Aid," *Adventist Review*, 15 June 1978, 16, 17.

CHAPTER 5

Angels Love Little People

"I have a miracle story for you," writes Kristi T., of Angwin, California.

My friend Connie was three years old and was playing on her tricycle. She rode out into the street just as a big car was coming. Suddenly a tall man appeared and picked her up and carried her to the sidewalk. Her mother turned around to thank the man, but he was already gone.

Then there was Jimmy. Jimmy lived in a little house on a cliff above the shores of beautiful Harrington Sound, on the island of Bermuda. The windows on the back side of the house were three stories above some sharp rocks leading down to the water.

One summer afternoon Jimmy took his nap in a back room, on a small bed near one of those windows. His father stayed with him for a while, and because the room was so hot and stuffy, he opened the window. But he forgot to close it when he went out.

When Jimmy woke up, he got out of the wrong side of the bed and fell through the window. His horrified father found him lying on the rocks below with a small cut on his head but no other sign of injury.

A fast trip to the hospital proved unnecessary. Apart from the cut, the doctors found nothing wrong. They all thought Jimmy was a very lucky little boy. Jimmy, however, had a far better explanation for his protection from harm. This is what he later told the nurses: "The angels caught me, and rested me down; that's why I didn't get hurt."[1]

Angels seem to love little people. Not that they don't love big ones too, but they have a special place in their heart for children's innocent naivete, which often leads them into danger. Jesus said, "See that you do not look down on one of these little ones. For I tell you that their angels in heaven always see the face of my Father in heaven" (Matthew 18:10).

This story comes from Pete C., of Simi Valley, California:

Our family was visiting an old church in Santa Barbara, California. There was a park across from the church. We had made lunch, so we went to the park for our picnic.

At the time, our family was Danny, nine years old; Kathy, seven; Anthony, five; and Theresa, three years old; with mother

Tonya and father Pete.

We started our picnic. The children were playing; lunch was ready. We all began to sit down at the picnic table. Anthony, our five-year-old, was not around. We looked and looked for him. Someone spotted him by a fountain near the street, a good seventy-five yards away, headed toward the street. There was no way we could reach him before he reached the street.

We asked our guardian angel to help us—to please go and get Anthony before he ran into the busy street.

To our surprise, as soon as we asked, Anthony's right hand went straight up into the air, and he went around the fountain and headed toward us—hand held high.

We ran toward him. Just as we arrived, his hand went down.

Sometimes children can see angels when adults cannot. Carey G., of Greenfield Park, Quebec, sent us this story:

Last summer at night during a terrible thunder and lightning storm, my daughter Sarah, age eleven, was terrified to the point of sheer panic. We were all in my bed together—Sarah, myself, my husband, and our little boy Jonathan (eight years).

We prayed and talked about God's protection. Jonathan, myself, and my husband settled down to sleep, but Sarah, still in a panic, couldn't sleep. Suddenly she sat bolt upright and said, "Look at the beautiful angel sitting on the side of the bed."

We were almost asleep and didn't move quickly, but even when we did, we couldn't see anything. But Sarah was adamant that there was an angel sitting beside her. She relaxed and fell asleep quickly. When she needed it most, God showed her that her guardian angel was close by, protecting her.

She still tells us about how radiant the angel was, with such golden hair and a glowing face.

Judy H. writes from Portland, Oregon, and tells a heart-warming story that happened when her son was about two years old. Their church was having a special seminar on worship. Toward the end of the service, her son pointed toward the speaker and said, "Angel, I see angel."

Judy and her husband questioned him: "Where is he?"

"Behind the speaker."

"What color is he wearing?"

"White."

"Is he bigger than the speaker?"

"Yes."

Later on they asked him if the angel was still there. "Yes," he said.

Over the following years they would ask Vic if he still remembered seeing the angel, and he still does to this day in his early twenties.

Here's a similar story from Stanley A. in Lawrenceville, Georgia:

> I wanted to tell you what the Lord Jesus Christ my Saviour has done. On June 6, 1985, my daughter Tracie (birthday July 15, 1982) was diagnosed as having leukemia.
>
> On the following Sunday night (June 11, at 11:30 p.m.) in the hospital, I was reading the Bible to Tracie, when all of a sudden Tracie started crying, and I said to her, "Why are you crying?"
>
> She answered, "I am scared."
>
> I told her that Jesus and His angels were protecting her, and she said, "No, He isn't."
>
> With that, I prayed the following prayer (silently), "Lord, let her see Your angels."
>
> No sooner had I prayed than Tracie started laughing and looking all around the room. I asked what was wrong now, and she said that she saw "Jesuses."
>
> I was very surprised and asked how many were there. Tracie said, "The room is full."

Then I asked her what they looked like, and Tracie said they were "big and pretty."

I then asked where the closest one was. Tracie turned to the right side of the bed and acted like she was feeling something, and then did the same on the left side.

Within five minutes, Tracie was sound asleep, and for the first time in five nights she did not wake up in pain.

The next day I read Psalm 34:7 in the Bible: "The angel of the Lord encampeth round about them that fear him, and delivereth them" (KJV).

On Tuesday, June 14, we brought Tracie home from the hospital. When we got home, Tracie brought me the Bible and asked me to "read me Jesus." I read the following in John 11:4: "This sickness is not unto death, but for the glory of God, that the Son of God might be glorified thereby" (KJV).

On Friday, June 21, the doctors at Emory University told us that Tracie was in remission.

Stanley wrote to us in 1990, testifying that Tracie was by then eight years old and still healthy. He believes she was cured by God. In closing his letter, Stanley asked us to please help him glorify the Lord by sharing this experience with others. Well, Stanley, consider the Lord glorified.

Dusty D., of Salem, New Hampshire, sent us two wonderful stories of God's love for children.

Many years ago when my husband and I started out raising a family, we lived in a small trailer in Burlington, Iowa. We didn't have very much room, so my husband and I had our bedroom in the living room, and my daughter Chali slept in the small bedroom located in the back of the trailer.

IN THE PRESENCE OF ANGELS

One night I put Chali, then only three years old, to bed with a fever. She hadn't felt good all day. Early in the morning, I heard her talking, so I quickly jumped out of bed. When I arrived, I asked her if everything was all right. She replied, "Everything is just fine. A little girl all shiny and bright told me that I'm going to get better and not to worry." Chali was too young to make up a story, and her description was definitely one of an angel.

I went back to the bedroom with my knees knocking. I told my husband what had just happened, and he suggested that I go back to check on her.

No way! I figured she was in good hands.

The next morning Chali told us again what happened. I think that it was wonderful for God to send a small angel, not some huge, tall angel that might have frightened a little three-year-old. Our Saviour was concerned about a little girl's fears of being sick. Praise God for His concern and love for the smallest of His family.

I also have some friends, Gary and Susie C., of Eaton, Ohio, whose daughter not only saw an angel but talked and sang songs with one.

When Susie's daughter had a very serious eye infection, Susie didn't know where she was going to get the money to take her daughter to a doctor. While out on an errand one day, she left her daughter home alone. An angel appeared and asked the daughter if she would like to go for a walk. They walked together down the rather long driveway that was part of the family's country home. As they walked, they talked and sang beautiful songs together. When they got to the end of the driveway, the angel said he would have to leave.

When Susie got home, her daughter told her what had happened. She said she was not at all afraid but had a feeling of peace and joy. Of course, Susie believed her, because her eye had been completely healed!

It was Christmas 1991. Michaele M. was living in Rainbow City, Alabama, and her oldest daughter, Jessica, was three. She put her other two babies, Katie, nineteen months, and Jacob, seven months, into a double stroller, and off she went to finish her Christmas shopping, Jessica in tow.

The mall was crowded. One moment Jessi was at her side, and the next moment she was gone. She began yelling frantically, "Jessi, Jessi!" and attracted quite a bit of attention.

"What did she have on?" bystanders asked. "What does she look like?" "How old is she?" Management paged for a lost child over the store loudspeaker.

Ten minutes passed . . . fifteen minutes. Michaele knew Jessi never talked to strangers—not even to people Michaele knew but Jessi didn't. In fact, Michaele felt sometimes that her Jessi was rather rude to people with this "stranger" thing!

After twenty minutes, a church friend walked up and offered to stay with Katie and Jacob while Michaele went out into the mall to look for Jessi. Suddenly Michaele remembered that all the way to the mall, Jessica had asked to see Santa. That's where she was! Michaele continues the story:

As I broke into a run through the mall, I saw my baby walking toward me with a smile on her face, holding some man's hand! It was an older man with a white beard and a sweet face. I really began to lose it by this time. Tears were streaming down my face. "Thank You, God! Thank You, God!"

I asked Jessi why she had gone out of the store and why she had gone with a stranger when she didn't even like them. She stopped me in midsentence. "But, Mommy, he wasn't a stranger. That was Gran's uncle, and he knew my name."

"No, Jessica, it was not Gran's uncle." Jessi insists it was to this day. My mother-in-law's eighty-year-old uncle lives in

Tampa, Florida, and was not in that mall.

I believe now that an angel appeared (in disguise) so that Jessi would feel comfortable enough to go with him back to me. Jessi was almost to the other end of the mall when he walked up to her and said, "Jessica, are you looking for your mommy? Come with me—I know where she is."

That night, as I lay down to sleep and thought about the events of the day, I thanked God. I believe to this day it was an angel sent from God to help me find my baby. I thank God for angels.

Most of the stories in this chapter are told by the parents. Here is one told by the child, now grown up, who saw an angel. It happened to Leona C., of Ontario, Oregon.

When I was a toddler, we lived in Camas, Washington. My mother had recently spent a long time in the hospital with a serious illness. She was getting dinner for my father and grandpa, who were hauling hay from a field between the house and the barn with an iron-wheeled wagon and team of horses.

My mother did not notice me slip out of the house to see my daddy and grandpa. The men didn't notice me either, as they pulled the last load of hay into the barn. Somehow I got caught between the wagon and the door of the barn. My daddy spied me just as the wagon ran over me. The wheel ran across me at an angle from my hips to my chest. My father picked me up and ran with me to the house, laying me on the bed, telling my mother not to let me move, that I must be crushed. You could see the wheel mark across me. But, thank God, no bones were broken. I just wanted to get down and play. Yet that load of hay was so heavy, being the last load of the day, that it broke the horses' harness when they pulled it into the barn.

My mother and father always had family worship every night and morning, asking God's protection for their family. They believed it was my guardian angel who lifted the wheel of the wagon. A few years later Leona actually saw an angel:

I was eight years old at the time, and we lived at Battle Ground, Washington. My father was a patient at the Portland Sanitarium. He had pneumonia and was not expected to live. My mother and we four children were home very sick with the flu. I was able to help care for the other children to some extent.

My mother was always very sick when we were growing up. At this particular time, we were all sleeping downstairs, where we had a potbelly stove on which we kept a teakettle for hot water. My two little brothers were just across the room from my bed, in bed with my mother. In the night my mother called, "Leona, you better get up and fill the water bottle for Verlin." He was sleeping just through the archway from our room on the sofa. I did and went back to my bed and closed my eyes.

I opened them again to see this beautiful angel looking down at my mother and my brothers Archie and Daryl. The angel was as bright as a light. How beautiful it was! I'll never forget that night. The angel was gliding back and forth across the bed, looking down at them.

I called, "Mama, there's something on your bed!" As I did, the angel glided off the bed, onto the rug, and into the other room. When I told Mother what I saw, she said, "It's our guardian angel watching over us."

To think that my eyes were opened to see an angel has always been a blessing to me.

IN THE PRESENCE OF ANGELS

As wonderful as these stories are, however, a note of caution is in order. Not all spirits that appear to children are holy angels. Many children have invisible playmates that are just an invention of their fertile imagination, but occasionally these imaginary playmates aren't so imaginary. An invisible playmate may also be an evil angel.

For example, we received a letter from a man by the name of Buck who related the sad story of a childhood acquaintance with a playmate entity that called himself "Bime Jime," whom he knew to be an evil spirit. To make a long story short, Buck spent the rest of his life in a struggle with alcoholism, and when he gave his life to Jesus, the demons did not let him go without a struggle.

How can you tell the true from the false? We'll discuss this at length later, but judging by the hundreds of angel stories we are familiar with, real angels do not ordinarily appear to us over an extended period of time, but only in brief, once-or-twice-in-a-lifetime moments of sickness, discouragement, or crisis.

However, in many spiritistic societies, it is common for children to grow up with spirit helpers.

Joe Poomaihealani is a descendant of a long line of native Hawaiians living on the island of Kauai. When he was a small boy, his mother was told in a dream of something special placed for her on a certain beach. The next day she found two stones on this beach shaped vaguely like a man and a woman. She took them home and placed them on an altar shelf in her bedroom. Instinctively, she knew they were *Ku'ulas*—fish gods, a brother and a sister. She left them offerings of small pieces of fruit and glasses of whiskey.

Joe's mother named these gods "Mokihanas." They belonged to Joe. They would travel with Joe as visible balls of fire whenever he went fishing. At the ocean, the Mokihanas would float or bounce out over the water to indicate where the fish were. He would cast his net underneath where they were dancing over the waves, always with good results.

Among traditional Hawaiians, *Ku'ulas* are generally believed to bring good luck, though they are sometimes used to bring trouble upon enemies. Each has its own special power. Curiously Joe's *Ku'ulas* liked to drink alcohol. After his marriage, Joe acquired other spirits that lived with him and sometimes made themselves visible.

Later, Joe and his wife studied the "Voice of Prophecy" Bible course lessons and decided to be baptized. His *Ku'ulas* disappeared, but only after a spiritual confrontation.[2] These *Ku'ulas* had real power and were generally benign to Joe up until the time he decided to give his life to the Lord. In the end, it was clear that they were evil spirits.

Johanna Michaelsen, in her book *Like Lambs to the Slaughter*, quotes Knud Rasmussen (1879-1933), a famous anthropologist and explorer who was recognized as an unrivaled authority on the Eskimo people. He reported an intriguing conversation with a former East Greenland shaman who had turned his back on shamanism after his conversion to Jesus Christ. This is what the former shaman said:

> I had many helping spirits who often were very useful to me, especially when I was exposed to gales or storms; and not many dangers could threaten me, because I felt safe. When later on I made up my mind to be baptized, they revealed themselves to me and advised me not to; however, I did what I had decided to do. Now I have been a baptized man for several years, and my old helping spirits have never visited me since, because I betrayed them by being baptized.[3]

In other words, invisible spirits are not all one happy family. Some of them love and worship Jesus Christ; others are His avowed enemies (though they will sometimes lie about this when it suits their purpose). Not all so-called "guardian angels" are on God's side—even when their relationship with children seems harmless.

When I (Lonnie) traveled in Australia a couple of years ago, I met a man named Gordon Lee, a long-time missionary in the Solomon Islands of the South Pacific. He shared some absolutely chilling stories from his experience. These events are very real in his part of the world, where animism, spiritism, and demon worship are such a part of everyday life. I remember in particular one thing he said to me: "Lonnie, I wouldn't even tell some of the stories to Western audiences, because they wouldn't believe them! But over there, young children are so steeped in this type of experience with the spirit world that it's a common thing to see them one moment playing in their playgrounds and the next moment being suspended in midair, as though resting in the lap of someone. They talk to and are caressed by this 'someone.' Then they jump down from this 'lap' and run back to the swings."

The spirit world is very real.

Johanna Michaelsen tells of a young girl who was visited in bed one night, when she was about six or seven, by an angelic being. It was a radiantly beautiful being full of soft, shining light. "I am an angel sent from Jesus," it told her. The child was from a deeply committed Christian family, and she loved Jesus. And yet she was terribly afraid at the presence of the "angel."

"You're *not* from Jesus!" the little girl challenged.

"How do you know?" responded the still-shining angel.

"Because in the Bible, every *real* angel said, 'Be not afraid' if someone was afraid of him. I'm afraid now, and you didn't say that to me!"

Instantly the being changed into a hideous manifestation that swooped down upon her. "Would you rather see me like this?" the thing hissed as it vanished into the dark behind her. The demon had been challenged and unmasked by a little child. Even at her tender age, her parents had trained her to be discerning. Even small children can be told about Jesus and the Bible and can put the spirits to the test.[4]

---

1. Alice Hill, *Adventist Review,* 29 July 1993, p. 11.
2. Gail Walker, *Spirits in His Parlor* (Boise, Idaho: Pacific Press, 1980).
3. From an article edited from posthumous notes left by Knud Rasmussen, "The Shaman's Magic Drum," *Shaman's Drum: A Journal of Experiential Shamanism,* Summer 1985, 22.
4. *Like Lambs to the Slaughter* (Eugene: Harvest House Publishers, 1989), 161, 162.

CHAPTER

6

Masquerade

It may be a passing fad, but currently Americans are obsessed with angels. They are the topic of movies, television programs, and bestsellers. In fact, even now, two weeks before Christmas as I (Lonnie) review this manuscript aboard a new Boeing 767 before sending it to the press, a movie about angels is playing on the screen. I'm not making this up. It's called *Angels in the Outfield*, a farcical tale about the California Angels baseball team.

The angels in this slapstick comedy are certainly

harmless enough. Indeed, most angels in the current crop of books and movies are all sweetness and light, as if every invisible spirit in the world wanted nothing but our good. This is a dangerous assumption, for all spirits are not alike. God's Word says that Satan masquerades as an angel of light (see 2 Corinthians 11:14). He and his infernal legions are masters of gentle imposter, beguiling alias, and deadly deceit.

There are even books in print today that purport to tell you how to get in contact with your angel, using methods that are basically occult in nature. If you try it, the spirit you make contact with may not be exactly what you had in mind! Curiosity has killed more than cats.

Holy angels cannot be summoned by any ritual. They only rarely appear to human beings, usually only in moments of crisis. They do not have an ongoing visible relationship with an individual unless that individual happens to be a prophet called by God, like John the apostle, who was given repeated visions and revelations to pass on to God's people. Rarely does anyone encounter an angel more than once in a lifetime, though they are near us every day.

Even though angels are sent to minister to us, they are under God's direction, not ours. There may be no harm in thanking our angels and praising God with them, but it is a mistake to pray to angels. After all, why speak to the underlings when you can speak directly to the Boss? In the Bible, angels are *sent* (see Daniel 3:28; 6:22; 10:11; Luke 1:19, 26) by God; they do not simply *come* on their own initiative, and they are never *summoned* by human beings (it is the superior who summons the inferior). We pray only to God, and sometimes He sends an angel to answer that prayer.

Holy angels never accept worship. Scripture warns against those who promote the worship of angels (see Colossians 2:18). When Manoah offered to honor the angel who visited him, the angel replied, "If you prepare a burnt offering, offer it to the Lord" (Judges 13:16). John the Revelator was so overwhelmed by what his guiding angel was showing him in vision that he impulsively fell at his feet in worship. In fact, he made the same mistake twice (see Revelation 19:10; 22:8, 9). Both times, the angel's horrified reaction was, in essence, "Don't do that! I'm just one of your brothers. I'm a servant of God as you are. God is the only One who deserves worship."

Notice the humility. Angels consider themselves our brothers—a heart-warming thought. They humble themselves; they exalt Jesus Christ and worship Him. When Jesus was born, God commanded all of the angels to worship Him (see Hebrews 1:6). Jesus now sits at God's right hand—with angels, authorities, and powers in submission to Him (see 1 Peter 3:22). If you ever encounter a spirit, put it to the test by asking, "Do you worship Jesus Christ of Nazareth, the Son of God?" (The name *Jesus* alone is not enough; both men and demons bear that name.)

Holy angels are exceptionally modest. They almost never talk about themselves; in fact, they seldom say much at all. This is one of the most striking aspects of the hundreds of modern angel stories we have dealt with. It's the same way in the Bible. Angels generally refuse to reveal their names, even when asked (see Genesis 32:29; Judges 13:17, 18). In all of the biblical angel appearances, only once does an angel introduce himself by name: Gabriel, in Luke 1:19. Only one other holy angel—Michael—is named in Scripture (the Apocrypha adds Raphael). The Apocalypse names the demonic angel of the abyss, Abaddon or Apollyon (see Revelation 9:11); the rest of its angels remain nameless; some are numbered, others described according to their function.

True angels of God never exalt themselves or babble on about "knowing all things." They shrink from anything that even remotely resembles pride, since that was the downfall of Lucifer, the morning star (see Isaiah 14:12-20). They are sent by God to accomplish a specific task, and once that task is accomplished, they rarely wait around for thanks.

Finally, angels are not spirits of the dead who have gone on to some advanced existence. Angels existed before any human being had ever died. Genesis 3:24 mentions that God placed cherubim, a type of angel, at the east of the Garden of Eden with flaming swords to guard the tree of life. This happened before the death of Adam and Eve, the first human beings.

Not only are angels not advanced human beings, but those apparitions that masquerade as spirits of the dead are in fact fallen angels. The dead cannot return or communicate with us (Ecclesiastes 9:5, 6; Job 7:9, 10; 2 Samuel 12:23). Those who think they are communicating with the dead are in fact communicating with demons, which is why God places this practice under a curse (Deuteronomy 18:9-12; Isaiah 8:19, 20).

So true angel appearances tend to fall into certain patterns. If you think you may have encountered an angel, consider the biblical characteristics mentioned above before deciding whether or not it was a heavenly messenger.

Let's examine a case study: a spirit by the name of Ramtha, who claims to be the thrity-five-thousand-year-old spirit of a dead warrior. J. Z. Knight, who has written a book about her experience with Ramtha entitled *A State of Mind, My Story*, claims that he comes and speaks to her often. In fact, in New Age circles, she is known as Ramtha's "channel." Knight's book about her encounters with Ramtha is full of foul language, which gives us our first clue as to the origin of Ramtha, for the wisdom that comes from heaven is first of all pure (see James 3:17). The second clue is found in what Ramtha says when he first appears to Knight:

> "Now beloved woman, you will be able to hear my words and, indeed, see my presence as no one else can. For I am Ramtha, the Enlightened One, the power that walks with you. Do not be in fear, for that which be I, be I of the I Am, and that be the I Am of God the Father, as you term it, indeed!"[1]

"Indeed, beloved entity, I know what you know.... That which be I, be God ... All is. Unto this understanding that I have given you, the only difference between you, beloved woman, and I, Ramtha, the Enlightened One, is that I, indeed, know that I am God and you do not know that you also be God. For then, that which know I, indeed, be All that I am, for know I All.[2]

In this discourse, Ramtha claims to be God, blasphemously appropriating to himself the title of God, "I Am." Moreover, he claims that J. Z. Knight is also God. There is no point in belaboring the standard Christian objections for those who do not share biblical presuppositions; yet it should be obvious to anyone, regardless of presuppositions, that Ramtha does not act like the angels mentioned in the Bible.

However, for those who do not accept the Bible as an authority, there is clue number three. Ramtha's claim to know all things can be tested empirically. For one thing, he does not know how to speak correct English. His tortured syntax is obviously a ploy to give the appearance of someone who comes from another culture. In fact, he appears to be unfamiliar with some of the most mundane matters of everyday life in the following exchange between Knight and Ramtha:

[Knight:] "I have to go to Safeway." With that, I picked up the dirty clothes and headed to the laundry chute, down the hall.

Ramtha, on my heels, asked, "What be a Safeway?"

I opened the chute and threw the clothes down into the abyss. "It's a market where you buy groceries."

"Groceries?"

I turned on my heel and headed toward Chris's room. "Yeah, you know, you probably used to come into a village and go down to the marketplace and trade things for your brazier, didn't you? I mean, after you conquered the place?" . . .

"Ahh, the purchasing of foodstuffs. Indeed. That be a Safeway?"

"Yeah, that be a Safeway."[3]

An all-knowing spirit with thirty-five thousand years of experience who hasn't figured out what groceries are? Not likely. Earlier Ramtha told J. Z., "I know what you know," so why doesn't he know about Safeway?

Those dirty clothes are not the only thing she should have sent to the abyss!

Obviously, "Ramtha" has made fools out of a lot of people who have paid big bucks to attend seminars to hear what he has to say through his channel. Ramtha is not what he claims to be. He is not the spirit of an ancient human warrior; he is a fallen angel, cast out of heaven for rebellion, along with Satan.

Demons are ego-stroking liars. Their leader, Satan, is called the father of lies in John 8:44. They are the defeated rebels, refugees from an ancient revolt in heaven described in Revelation 12:7-9:

> There was war in heaven. Michael and his angels fought against the dragon, and the dragon and his angels fought back. But he was not strong enough, and they lost their place in heaven. The great dragon was hurled down—that ancient serpent called the devil or Satan, who leads the whole world astray. He was hurled to the earth, and his angels with him.

It would have been nice if Satan had gone somewhere else; but no, he came down here to planet Earth to continue his rebellion against God. Genesis 3 tells how Satan brought sin and death into this perfect world God had created by using a serpent as his channel to tempt Eve to sin.

Nowadays Satan is being rehabilitated. In some angel books he is portrayed as a being whose motives have been "misunderstood." It is suggested that evil is the necessary opposite of good, without which good could not exist; thus Satan is the balancing force, or requisite polarity, to God.

It's all a massive disinformation campaign to transform Satan into an angel of light. Meanwhile, he and his hellish minions are still fomenting hatred, racial conflict, and egomania. And they still love to receive human worship. So don't blindly follow any spirit being, no matter how wonderful he, she, or it may appear.

If holy angels cannot be summoned by any ritual, other, less desirable spirits certainly can be!

All Matthew Hensley wanted was to get his sweetheart back. His girlfriend had just told him that their relationship was over. In his aimless wanderings, he found himself in a bookstore, where he spotted a bright red book whose jacket proclaimed that it would make him rich and famous or give him whatever he wanted—if only he would use the right spell and follow the ritual. Matthew's curiosity was aroused. He bought it on a whim, not really believing its claims, but as he leafed through it over dinner, he came to a section that claimed to be able to win back lost girlfriends. Aha! Suddenly he began reading in earnest.

His reading led him into an apparently silly ritual involving various bizarre objects and the recitation of certain words. The next day he took the day off, procured the objects, and went through the ritual.

The following day his girlfriend called. She asked him if they could have dinner together. That evening she came to his house. It was wonderful—it seemed the spell had worked! She was radiant.

They kissed. Then the doorbell rang, but there was no one there. Then the pounding began; the lights; the noises; the plug wires pulled out of place in the car—a nightmare of strange events. Blasphemous words written in a foul-smelling substance were smeared on the walls. Unplugged radios played by themselves.

Eventually Matthew called a priest, who called in an expert on the paranormal, Captain Kevin Randle, who explained to Matthew that he was being troubled by a demonic spirit. "What did you do to invite the spirit in here?" he said.

"I didn't do anything. It just began to happen," said Matthew, who wasn't a Christian and was genuinely puzzled by all that had happened.

"No," said Captain Randle, "it doesn't just happen. Have you been using a Ouija board? A book on witchcraft? Performing rituals? Reading the satanic bible? There has to be something."

Matthew admitted he had performed a ritual. Randle went on to explain to him that he was troubled by a lesser demon, for a more powerful one might have possessed him instead of merely harassing him. Eventually the demon was induced to depart, and Matthew and his girlfriend got married.[4]

Yes, it's a true story. Matthew didn't set out to get involved with the occult. All he was looking for was a shortcut—a shortcut to love. He had no idea what was behind the door he was opening.

There are other shortcuts. Lots of them. Human beings like shortcuts. The problem with shortcuts is that you can get lost on the way. They may take you where you don't want to go. Believe me, the occult is not just a farce. There is power in it—deadly power. And curiosity can kill more than cats.

Let's do a little history. There have been outbreaks of the supernatural for thousands of years. In America, there was a spirit entity with a female voice that unmercifully harassed the Bell family of Tennessee for years, beginning in 1817. It predicted the Civil War before finally disappearing.

But organized spiritualism in America began in the home of the Fox sisters, Margaret and Kate, in 1848. On March 31 of that year, in the secluded village of Hydesville, New York, the sisters heard a mysterious rapping in the walls of the house they were staying in. They soon established a code of communication with the spirits. "Mr. Splitfoot," as they called the rapper, could rap out the number of fingers they were holding up. It could rap out the number of children born to Mrs. Fox, including one who had died. The entity eventually claimed to be the spirit of a murdered peddler whose body had been buried in the cellar.

The rappings became a sensation and soon spread all over New York State. The Fox sisters were accused of fraud, but when it became clear that no fraud was involved, spiritism grew by leaps and bounds. By 1854, six years later, the movement had spread to every part of the United States and parts of Europe. Ten years later, thirty thousand mediums were practicing in the United States. The eleventh edition of *Encyclopaedia Britannica* states that spiritism "spread like an epidemic."

The Fox sisters rose to prominence, but they later became alcoholics. They claimed that the spirits had promised them protection, but it never came. As their craving for alcohol increased, they lost all sense of moral responsibility. In 1888, at an anti-spiritualist meeting, Margaret declared, "I am here tonight, as one of the founders of spiritualism, to denounce it as absolute false-hood . . . the most wicked blasphemy the world has ever known." Both mediums died cursing God.

Unfortunately, most modern-day dabblers in the occult have yet to learn the horrible lessons the Fox sisters and Matthew Hensley learned. Today, a medium is called a "channeler." The search for shortcuts to power goes on, and millions of people are destined to find out that their shortcuts are doors into hell.

Spiritism and New Age philosophy are much older than the Fox sisters. It all began in the first conversation between Eve and the serpent in Eden, described in Genesis chapter 3. God had told Eve that if she ate of the fruit, she would die. But the serpent told Eve, "You will not surely die. . . . For God knows that when you eat of it your eyes will be opened, and you will be like God, knowing good and evil" (verse 4).

The serpent claimed the fruit was an open door into higher consciousness. He made two claims: you won't die, and you will be as God. These two deceptions are the principal tenets of New Age philosophy, which is a recycled form of spiritism. When Eve accepted this philosophy and ate the fruit, it brought death and suffering and pain into the world. Her curiosity killed. Instead of being lifted into realms of higher consciousness, human beings were degraded and debased.

Notice something about this little episode in the garden. When the serpent propounded his philosophy, all the evidence was on his side. It was obvious that this snake had indeed found a path to higher consciousness and supernatural powers, because he was demonstrating it before Eve's very eyes. Snakes don't talk, but this one did! The only evidence Eve had to the contrary was the word of God.

The point is that it is best to trust God's Word, even when so-called scientific evidence seems to point temporarily in another direction—even when an alleged thirty-five-thousand-year-old dead warrior materializes in your bedroom as living "proof" of the claims of spiritism.

Why are these two satanic tenets from Eden—no death and every person a god—so important to Satan? Well, think about it. If these things are true, then live as you please. You have forever to reform. If not now, then in some future, higher realm of existence. And why reform at all if you are god? Gods make their own rules.

Can you imagine what the world would be like if everyone believed they made their own rules and were answerable to no one? If you want to know what happens when people who believe this acquire power, just take an inventory of recent wars.

And another thing. If people believe that the spirits of the dead can bring secrets from beyond the grave, then Satan can use this channel to propagate his lies as though they were the wisdom of the ages. And he is doing so.

Elisabeth Kubler-Ross is widely known as the author of several books on death. What is not so widely known is that she is a medium, or channel, through whom a spirit by the name of Salem speaks—a spirit much like Ramtha.

In any large bookstore today, you can find books in the occult section that were dictated by spirits. Some of the most popular are those by Jane Roberts. A spirit entity who identified himself as Seth dictated millions of words to her, and her works have sold millions. Since her death in 1984, others have been used by Seth as channels for his deceptions.

It is one thing for angels to intervene in moments of danger, and quite another for them to start imparting information in a systematic way. Be extremely wary of books that invite you to "ask your angels." When you do, you will probably get an answer—but from whom?

Entire belief systems have been founded on alleged angelic revelations. Islam is founded on the revelations of the angel Jibril (Arabic for Gabriel) to Muhammad, and Mormonism on the revelations of the angel Moroni to Joseph Smith. But Galatians 1:8 says, "Even if we or an angel from heaven should preach a gospel other than the one we preached to you, let him be eternally condemned!" And 1 John 4:1-3 warns us to test the spirits, because there are many false prophets in the world.

Sorcery need not be witches dancing around a caldron or seances in the dark or rappings on a wall. Sometimes it appears in garments of light.

Richard Bach wrote the bestseller *Jonathan Livingston Seagull.* It's a beautiful and inspiring story about a precocious seagull. But this book and Bach's later writings are full of New Age philosophy and were inspired by a spirit, according to Bach's own testimony. The same is true of inspirational self-help books by Napoleon Hill and other writers. Such books play on our lust for power, knowledge, success. New Age theory offers shortcuts to self-esteem. "Unleash the powers that are within you," they say. "Realize your divinity."

Then there are near-death experiences (NDEs), in which people who have suffered traumatic, life-threatening injuries or disease lose consciousness for a time and then awaken with stories of having approached the gates of heaven, only to be given the opportunity to return to earth. Some researchers estimate that as many as seven million people in North America have had an NDE. Out-of-the-body experiences are as old as the Bible—Paul describes one in 2 Corinthians 12—and as new as the latest bestseller list. The movie *The Wizard of Oz* is a classic tale of an imaginary NDE. But today, NDEs have become big business. At first, they were just interesting phenomena; now, they have become sources of truth. An extended NDE can make you a prophet, an expert on God, a guru to millions.

Betty Eadie is a Mormon and a former hypnotherapist. One day, she claims, her spirit left the hospital bed her body was lying in, and the details of the experience that followed occupy over one hundred pages in her book *Embraced by the Light*.[5]

This book stayed at the top of the New York Times bestseller list for over a year. In it, Eadie describes how she was given a guided tour through heaven and learned many wonderful things. The book has much to say about love and the importance of serving others. Without love, she writes, we are nothing. Alongside such warm fuzzies, she serves up a potpourri of New Age tenets and Mormonism.[6]

While in heaven, Eadie encountered a surpassingly brilliant being of unconditional love whom she believed to be Jesus Christ, who gently said to her, "Your death was premature, it is not yet your time."[7] Then she was given a sort of "graduation" party by a group of angelic beings wearing soft pastel gowns to show her what she would receive when she returned at the right time. When they realized Betty didn't want to go back yet, they allowed her to travel to distant galaxies and meet other children of God.

Now, this suggests a problem based, not on the Bible, but on common sense. Are we to believe that God allows people to be mistakenly admitted into heaven? Perhaps His book-keeping system needs updating. And if Betty was there prematurely, why was she given such royal treatment, when she shouldn't have been there at all?

Or was Eadie's vision a clever counterfeit?

The teachings of Betty Eadie put her into a class with the biblical "soothsayers," people who teach soothing things, who comfort the comfortable. That is one reason such books are bestsellers. They pander to the sort of people who said to the biblical prophets, "Give us no more visions of what is right! Tell us pleasant things, prophesy illusions. Leave this way, get off this path, and stop confronting us with the Holy One of Israel!" (Isaiah 30:10, 11). And their message involves no restrictions, no self-denial, no cross, no atonement, no sin, and no judgment; only endless self-advancement and loving acceptance of the lie.

It is always easier to believe a blissful lie than to be confronted with a holy God. So beware! Unlike modern oracles, the Bible has been tested over millennia and found trustworthy. And it predicts that "in later times some will abandon the faith and follow deceiving spirits and things taught by demons" (1 Timothy 4:1).

Falsehood assumes many forms. I (Tim) was reading another recently published book that purports to be an account of a series of visions. The author, a Christian, tells of her many journeys through hell, which she describes in great detail. As I continued to read, I came to a section in which the writer encountered some cherubim. The cherubim she saw were the cute, chubby little infants of late Western tradition, not the awesome majesties of the Bible. I immediately lost interest in the supposed visions of this woman. Both she and Betty Eadie may sincerely believe in their visions, but they are deceived.

Yes, even Christians can be duped. The most shocking thing is that they may even be using the power of Satan while believing they are working for Christ. Matthew 7:15-23 describes people who work miracles in Jesus' name (such as faith healing or exorcism) but are unwittingly caught up in a satanic counterfeit.

Beware the masquerade.

Scripture predicts an epidemic of satanic miracles near the end of time. Matthew 24:24 says, "False Christs and false prophets will appear and perform great signs and miracles to deceive even the elect—if that were possible." Revelation 16:14 says that in the end of time, just before the great Battle of Armageddon, the spirits of devils working miracles will go forth to deceive the whole world. Finally, this startling prediction from 2 Thessalonians 2:9, 10:

> The coming of the lawless one will be in accordance with the work of Satan displayed in all kinds of counterfeit miracles, signs and wonders, and in every sort of evil that deceives those who are perishing.

Satan is even now infiltrating the media with his philosophies that lead, step by step, to an astounding demonic omega. He seems to be planning a final deception whose initial movements are so subtle, so stealthy, that they don't even register on the church's spiritual radar screens.

Many intelligent people who do not believe in the supernatural *do* believe in the possibility of life from outer space. They have been programmed by movies such as the Star Wars trilogy, *Close Encounters of the Third Kind, 2010,* and the "Star Trek" television series. What better way for Satan to deceive the nations than to make them think that salvation from war and crime and starvation is coming from outer space in the form of an ancient and wise race of alien beings who will teach us how to live in peace and harmony?

Masquerade

All religions have prophecies of some messiah-like figure to come. Guess who is planning to show up as that messiah-like figure?

Several experts who have studied the subject extensively have become convinced that UFOs are spiritistic phenomena. Ships traveling at thousands of miles per hour suddenly change course at a ninety-degree angle. One ship splits into two. The ships change shape in midcourse. Those who claim to have been contacted by beings from these spacecraft experience strange harassment and poltergeist activity. And they receive the same messages that spirit mediums and psychics receive, including predictions of future catastrophes.

In 1970 former skeptic John Keel wrote a book called *UFOs: Operation Trojan Horse.* His conclusion: "The UFOs do not seem to exist as tangible, manufactured objects. They do not conform to the accepted natural laws of our environment. . . . The UFO manifestations seem to be, by and large, merely minor variations of the age-old demonological phenomenon" (299).

More recently, another pair of experts have reached similar conclusions. Nelson Pacheco and Tommy Blann have written a book called *Unmasking the Enemy.*[8] The authors are two highly qualified former air force men whose thesis is that UFOs are demonic. Pacheco, a Roman Catholic, and Blann, a Protestant, reached this conclusion after decades of studying such phenomena as crop circles and apparitions. The testimonies of hundreds of credible witnesses describe UFOs as "vanishing on the spot." Yet they also leave discernable physical effects, such as scars on abductees and radar tracks. The evidence indicates we are dealing with a spiritual phenomenon. Pacheco and Blann also place apparitions of the Virgin Mary in a similar category.[9]

Why are we talking about UFOs in a book on angels? Because we believe fallen angels are behind some UFO phenomena, and this is part of their strategy of deception. Remember that the Bible calls Satan "the ruler of the kingdom of the air" (Ephesians 2:2) and predicts great signs in the sky near the end of time (see Luke 21:11). I suspect Satan is conditioning humanity for an overwhelming surprise.

What is it all leading up to? What grand finale does Satan have in mind?

Someday soon, all the mediums and psychics and Ouija boards and apparitions of the Virgin Mary are going to start saying the same thing all at once: Christ is coming! He will appear at such and such a date, in a glorious spaceship. Or He'll meet with His followers on top of such and such a mountain.

I do not attend movie theaters, and I rarely rent videocassettes, but I (Tim) still remember watching the climactic scene in the movie *Close Encounters of the Third Kind* at home one night with my wife. In a very moving sequence near the end of the film, human beings make first contact with friendly aliens. Even though I suspected that I was watching a dress rehearsal for the grand deception the Bible predicts, I was nearly moved to tears. Powerful emotions swept over me as these benevolent beings of light and love linked arms with humanity to begin a new era of peace.

If a mere movie on a television screen could have that effect on me, then imagine the power the real thing will have on an ignorant populace! When the mastermind of evil assumes his final radiant disguise and steps out of a pulsating spaceship in dazzling splendor amidst "angelic" choirs and proclaims peace to all nations, I predict it will produce instant worldwide unity. The sick will be healed. Miracles worked. New "truths" revealed. And plumbers and politicians, mothers and murderers, weary of the struggle, will feel a sweet heart longing to believe that whatever he says is true. Who will want to listen to an old-fashioned Book that, for two thousand years, has brought, not peace, but a sword?

God help us then!

A terrible delusion is about to come upon the world. The only way to escape it is to trust God's Word, and nothing else. If we will simply take God at His word, we will be safe. If not, then . . . well, curiosity has killed more than cats.

Since we have been so hard on Ramtha, let's give him the last word. It's only fair.

There is one fascinating piece of dialogue in J. Z. Knight's book in which an introspective Ramtha reveals his feelings about God. Could it be that, for once, Ramtha was telling the truth?

> [Knight:] "Is there anything you can't do?"
>
> Ramtha smiled and put the guitar back where he had picked it up. "I cannot feel my heart break in sorrow or my stomach clutch in fear. I am beyond that experience. I no longer desire it."
>
> "Do you ever cry?"
>
> "I weep for that which is a deep love."
>
> "A deep love of what?"
>
> "A deep love of God. It is a most poignant remembrance of the past. Indeed, my most exquisite memory." He then picked up a comic book—I think it was *Spider Man*—and started flipping through it. Then he continued, "Lady, there be no passion as deeply experienced as the love of God. None."[10]

Poor Ramtha. From celestial courts to comic books. From Seraph to Spider Man. From following God through the galaxies to following J. Z. Knight through the laundry. Ramtha is living with the tragic consequences of a horrible decision he made thousands of years ago, and he's trying to take as many with him as he can.

Millions are following Ramtha's lead in letting pride or selfish priorities steal their heart away from the One to whom it belongs and apart from whom it can never rest. What a tragedy! Take it from a being who's been there: you don't want to miss out on heaven! Don't let anything prevent you from experiencing the most incredible joy that exists in the universe: the joy of knowing and loving God and being loved by Him.

IN THE PRESENCE OF ANGELS

1. J. Z. Knight, *A State of Mind: My Story* (New York: Warner Books, 1987), 25, 26.

2. Ibid., 26, 27.

3. Ibid., 347.

4. Sharon Jurvis, *True Tales of the Unknown* (New York: Bantam Books, 1985), 47-72.

5. Placerville, Calif.: Gold Leaf Press, 1992.

6. Some of Eadie's questionable teachings: All religions on earth are valid and have something to teach us. Each microscopic part of plants and each drop of water have their own intelligence. We need to look within ourselves and trust our innate abilities when we are in need of help. Eve's partaking of the fruit in the garden was necessary to her progression; it freed her to have children. All of us were preexisting spirits at the moment of creation, and we all took part in creation; some of these spirits chose not to be born on earth but to serve as angels. People don't really die when they die; death is merely a transition. We should pray for the dead. All will eventually be saved. Some learn of Jesus Christ here on earth, others while in the spirit after their death. For a critical appraisal of Eadie's book, see Richard Abanes, *Embraced by the Light and the Bible* (Camp Hill, Penn.: Horizon Books, 1994).

7. Knight, 42.

8. Arlington, Va.: Bendan Press, 1994.

9. *Omni*, October 1994, 101.

10. Knight, 348.

CHAPTER

7

Invisible War, Invincible Warriors

Have you ever had anyone fight over you?

No?

Wrong answer!

There are invisible powers fighting over you right now. They are fighting for the right to determine your destiny. All of the stories in this book are examples of people who have found themselves caught in the age-old cross-fire between good and evil. This is no make-believe conflict. Every human being is a foot soldier in a great war that began in heaven eons ago. We are at the mercy of forces far more powerful than we, and neutrality is impossible. Those who consider themselves to be bystanders are in fact sleeping captives.

We may be pawns in a struggle between titans, but we are not helpless pawns. We have the freedom to choose sides with the rebels or the loyalists. And we have recourse to the weapon of prayer. Although the ultimate winner is not in doubt, yet the outcome of the battle in our locality depends very much on us.

Think of it this way: God and Satan are playing a cosmic game of Monopoly, for each wants a monopoly on the universe. Satan is seeking to demonstrate that his system is superior. But this grand demonstration, this deadly serious "game," must have some rules. Certain restrictions are placed upon Satan and his demonic angels. They cannot use their great power to simply kill someone, say, or burn down a house at will. Ordinarily they are not allowed to violate human freedom like this; instead, they must influence one of their human agents to do their bidding, or else their followers must invoke the demons' power.

God seems to operate under much the same self-imposed restrictions. Ordinarily He does not automatically intervene in miraculous ways unless His children ask Him in prayer. Prayer is a wonderful thing: it unlocks the power of God. This is why God sometimes impresses one of His children to pray just before some crisis is about to occur in the life of a loved one some distance away. Evidently God has ordained that supernatural powers cannot directly interfere in human affairs except by human permission. So whenever God intervenes to work a direct miracle, you can be sure that someone, somewhere, is praying.

One reason so many accidents happen without angelic intervention is that people forget to pray. Deliverance doesn't usually just happen automatically, not even for God's children. In most of the stories in this book, angels intervene only after someone calls upon God. Good or evil, the supernatural must be invited (recall the story of Matthew Hensley whose home was haunted after he tried to cast a spell). Those are the rules of the game.

The nature of this spiritual warfare, and the critical importance of prayer, is described in Ephesians 6:12-18:

> Our struggle is not against flesh and blood, but against the rulers, against the authorities, against the powers of this dark world and against the spiritual forces of evil in the heavenly realms. Therefore put on the full armor of God, so that when the day of evil comes, you may be able to stand your ground. . . . And pray in the Spirit on all occasions with all kinds of prayers and requests. With this in mind, be alert and always keep on praying for all the saints.

These principalities and powers, or demonic world rulers, are also mentioned in the Psalms. An early Greek translation of Psalm 96:4, 5 says, "For the Lord is great, and greatly to be praised; he is terrible above all gods. All the gods of the heathen are demons, but the Lord made the heavens." Psalm 97:7 says, "Worship him, all you gods!"

Yes, the Bible recognizes the existence of other "gods." Although they are not really self-existent deities at all, neither are they merely make-believe. They are fallen angels; powerful spirits who have rebelled against their Creator. The gods and goddesses of ancient times had their own prophets and their holy places where they could be consulted, such as the oracle at Delphi. Paul mentions in 1 Corinthians 10:20 that those who offer sacrifices to idols are offering them to demons.

These territorial gods and goddesses still exist today, and the worship of some of them is being revived in the West.

It seems that from ancient times Satan has divided up the world among his angels so that high-ranking principalities are assigned to oversee a nation and subordinate angels, to states, cities, and so forth. Demons are not omnipresent, and it seems to take them time to travel from one place to another. Hence they confine their

97

labors to a certain locality.

The ancients apparently understood some of these things. In 1 Kings 20:23-32 the story is told of the Arameans, whose capital was in Damascus. Israel had defeated them in battle in the hill country around Samaria. The king's advisors suggested that perhaps Israel's gods were gods only of the mountains, so the next year the king of Aram attacked the army of Israel in the plain, hoping his gods would be able to give him the victory there.

Of course, the God of the Bible, Israel's God, is not limited to any certain locality, and the Arameans learned this the hard way when they lost the battle and their king's advisors had to come crawling to Israel's king dressed in sackcloth, pleading for mercy.

The spiritual rulers of darkness against which we are fighting are powerful, but they are doomed by the blood of Jesus. Their ultimate fate is mentioned in the last part of Isaiah 24:21, 22:

> In that day [when the earth is destroyed] the Lord will punish the powers in the heavens above and the kings on the earth below. They will be herded together like prisoners bound in a dungeon; they will be shut up in prison and be punished after many days.

Notice that there are earthly kings and that there are invisible heavenly powers behind those kings. This helps us to understand Isaiah 14 and Ezekiel 28, which describe the origin of evil and the primordial fall of Satan. On the surface, these passages seem to be speaking of human rulers of historical empires. Yet the language is such that it can only apply to the "power behind the power," the spiritual ruler that stands behind the earthly king: Satan, the "prince of this world" (John 12:31; 14:30; 16:11).

Chapter 10 of the book of Daniel gives us the clearest glimpse into the spiritual warfare between territorial spirits in the Bible. After Daniel fasted and prayed for three weeks, the angel Gabriel appeared to him and said, in verses 12 and 13:

"Do not be afraid, Daniel. Since the first day that you set your mind to gain understanding and to humble yourself before your God, your words were heard, and I have come in response to them. But the prince of the Persian kingdom resisted me twenty-one days. Then Michael, one of the chief princes, came to help me, because I was detained there with the king of Persia."

Now this *prince* of Persia was a demonic being whose territory included Persia, as opposed to the *king* of Persia, who was a human being named Cyrus, known to historians as Cyrus the Great, the founder of the Persian Empire.

The angel explained to Daniel that he had been struggling against this demon for some time. It had cost Daniel three weeks of fasting and vigorous prayer. In the war between good and evil, victory is not effortless. Gabriel was not fighting a human foe, but perhaps Satan himself, and he was very nearly evenly matched. Daniel's prayers made the difference.

How can a fallen angel resist an angel of God? Consider the possibility that these spiritual warriors were fighting for control of the mind of the king, in which case victory would depend on his free-will decision.

Daniel's prayer seems to have been prompted by a political crisis. Not long before this, Cyrus had issued a decree (see Ezra 1:1-4) permitting all the exiled Jews to return to their homeland and to rebuild their temple in Jerusalem, as the prophet Jeremiah had predicted (chapters 25:11, 12; 29:10). About this time, some local opponents of the Jews had hired counselors to convince the king to stop all support for the rebuilding of the temple in Jerusalem. Evidently these counselors had been successful in convincing Cyrus to temporarily halt the reconstruction, and God's people became discouraged. This delay in building the temple is mentioned in the writings of the prophets Haggai and Zechariah and in Ezra 4:4, 5. So God sent Gabriel to counteract the forces of evil—

just as He sends angels to our aid when we ask Him.

This delay is evidently what Daniel was praying about. Dr. William Shea has done some fascinating research on this.[1] He discovered that Daniel's vision can be dated exactly. To translate the date into modern terminology, it took place on May 11, 535 B.C., which happened to be a Sabbath. Exactly three weeks before the angel visited, the day Daniel began his fast, was the very day that Cyrus's son Cambyses, the crown prince of Persia, succeeded to a new position of power that placed him in a position where he could oppose the rebuilding of the temple. This was also very close to the time when the foundation of the new temple was laid.

We know from Persian court records that Cambyses was opposed to foreign cults, and Daniel must have known this too. Indeed, we know through ancient records that not only the Jerusalem temple, but certain Egyptian temples as well, lay in ruins all during the reign of Cambyses. They were not rebuilt until after Darius took over the throne in 522 B.C. Work on the temple in Jerusalem resumed in 520 and was finally completed in 515 B.C.

So despite Daniel's prayers, the problem was not solved immediately. Gabriel's victory was only temporary, because Gabriel went on to say, in verse 20, "Soon I will return to fight against the prince of Persia, and when I go, the prince of Greece will come." Soon Gabriel would have to renew the battle with the principalities of darkness. But first he brought a message from God for Daniel that revealed to him the long ages of terrible struggle to come, followed by glorious victory in the end. This prophecy of the future occupies the final chapters of Daniel's book.

This spiritual warfare continues today; we are still fighting in the war that Daniel and Gabriel were engaged in.

The book *Wrestling With Dark Angels* relates an incident that took place in 1973. As Loren Cunningham of Youth With a Mission (YWAM) and twelve co-workers were praying and fasting for three days in Los Angeles, the Lord revealed to them that they should pray for the downfall of the prince of Greece. On the same day, similar groups in New Zealand and Europe received the same word. All three groups obeyed and engaged in the spiritual warfare of prayer against that principality. Within twenty-four hours, a political coup changed the government of Greece, and for the first time, YWAM workers could preach the gospel in the streets.[2]

Who knows what Promethean struggles were going on in the spiritual realms during the recent upheaval in the USSR? Perhaps it was the prayers of many humble Christians, and not the machinations of politicians, that brought freedom there.

This brings us to the subject of angel warriors. Contrary to popular opinion, even holy angels are not all sweetness and light. Sometimes they gird on their armor and fight as warriors in the ongoing war that began in heaven. Normally agents of God's mercy, they are also agents of His wrath; witness the seven angels of the apocalypse who are given the command, "Go, pour out the seven bowls of God's wrath on the earth" (Revelation 16:1) near the end of time.

The scriptural phrase *the Lord of Hosts* is a military term meaning "the commander of the armies." Joel implored God to "bring down your warriors, O Lord!" (Joel 3:11). "The chariots of God," writes the psalmist, "are tens of thousands and thousands of thousands" (Psalm 68:17). Against the Egyptians, God "unleashed . . . his hot anger, his wrath, indignation and hostility—a band of destroying angels" (Psalm 78:49).

A whole band of destroying angels must have awesome power, for a single angel is capable of wiping out a whole army. God promised the Israelites that He would "send an angel before you and drive out the Canaanites, Amorites, Hittites, Perizzites, Hivites and Jebusites" (Exodus 33:2). Later, when the nation of Israel was threatened with destruction by the Assyrian army, King Hezekiah fasted and prayed for God to deliver them. The result was that Hezekiah's army did not have to lift a finger:

> The angel of the Lord went out and put to death a hundred
> and eighty-five thousand men in the Assyrian camp. When

the people got up the next morning—there were all the dead bodies! (Isaiah 37:36; see also 2 Chronicles 32:21).

Though we usually think of angels as preserving life, sometimes they are authorized to take it. These destroying angels are pictured with sword in hand in 2 Samuel 24:16, 17; 1 Chronicles 21:15-30; and Numbers 22:23, 31. Their retribution was sometimes directed, not at Israel's enemies, but at Israel itself in times of apostasy. Paul in 1 Corinthians 10:10 reminded his Christian converts not to grumble as did some of the Israelites, who "were killed by the destroying angel." A few decades after Christ was born, King Herod met a similar fate:

> Immediately, because Herod did not give praise to God, an angel of the Lord struck him down, and he was eaten by worms and died (Acts 12:23).

Sometimes God even employs human mercenaries in His army; once, He used the Medes to accomplish the destruction of Babylon. Of these conquerors, God said, "I have commanded my holy ones; I have summoned my warriors to carry out my wrath—those who rejoice in my triumph" (Isaiah 13:3). Though the Medes (verse 17) were heathens, yet God called them "the weapons of his wrath" (verse 5) to punish Babylon (verse 19), whose time was up.

So sometimes God takes sides and sends His angels to fight alongside human soldiers. On rare occasions, they can even be seen.

In August of 1914, the German juggernaut had marched into the heart of Belgium, sweeping aside all resistance. The fighting between the Germans and the Belgian, French, and British forces was intense. The British Expeditionary Force had been fighting for days with no rest, and the men were on the verge of collapse. Word was carried back to Britain that the BEF, outnumbered three to one, was facing imminent defeat. The entire nation of Britain responded with prayer, filling the churches.

On August 26, a battle was fought near the city of Mons. At one particularly critical point in the battle, as the British were withdrawing through the city with the German cavalry hot on their heels, the intense artillery barrage suddenly fell silent. The British saw four or five white-robed beings, much larger than people, floating between them and the Germans. The angels had their backs to the British and their hands outstretched toward the Germans, as if to call them to a halt. The Germans abandoned the attack and began a chaotic retreat.

A number of British soldiers told essentially the same story. Reports were published by journalist Arthur Machen in the *London Evening News*; by an army chaplain, Rev. C. M. Chavasse; Captain Cecil Lightwick; and others. One lieutenant colonel described how, during the retreat, his battalion was escorted for twenty minutes by a squadron of phantom cavalry.

Despite overwhelming odds and heavy casualties, the Allied forces were able to successfully regroup and retreat to a well-dug-in defensive position.[3]

This was not the first time angels put in an appearance to stop an army. Second Kings chapter 6 tells how the king of Syria went to war with Israel and sent a great army with many chariots and horses to surround the city of Dothan and capture Elisha the prophet, a servant of God. When the prophet's servant got up early the next morning and went outside, he discovered that they were surrounded.

"Alas, my master, what shall we do now?" he cried out to Elisha.

"Don't be afraid!" Elisha told him. "For our army is bigger than theirs."

Then Elisha prayed, "Lord, open his eyes and let him see!" Suddenly, the servant saw horses and chariots of fire all over the mountain. They were protected by an army of angels.

Those invincible warriors still live today and surround those who fear God and deliver them, as promised in Psalm 34:7.

There are several well-known episodes of God's deliverance during World War II that might be discussed, such as the incredible rescue of the British Expeditionary Force at Dunkirk. But one of the most intriguing is the little-known story of the shining angel who intervened to save the Finns from Russian forces about midnight on December 24, 1939, at Taipale, on the Karelin Isthmus. Just as the Finnish army was about to run out of supplies and ammunition, a brilliant light brought all fighting to a halt. As the eyes of the soldiers adjusted to the light, they saw a shining angel holding a luminous cross that was pointed toward Finland. There was no more fighting that night; the exhausted soldiers slept after three days of continuous round-the-clock fighting, and supplies were brought in that turned the tide of battle.[4] This is quite similar to something God did for Israel at the Exodus:

> The angel of God, who had been traveling in front of Israel's army, withdrew and went behind them. The pillar of cloud also moved from in front and stood behind them, coming between the armies of Egypt and Israel. Throughout the night the cloud brought darkness to the one side and light to the other side; so neither went near the other all night long (Exodus 14:19, 20).

Five years after the Finnish miracle, General George Patton didn't need an angel; he only needed some blue sky.

When the Allied armies were poised on the borders of Germany, snowy weather grounded the American air force. The German general, von Rundstedt, attacked a weak point in the American lines at Ardennes. During that Christmas offensive of 1944, the fate of the Allied Expeditionary Force hung by a thread.

After days of continual gloomy weather, Patton walked into his map room in a furious temper and to the bewilderment of his staff began to speak firmly to God. "I need four days of fine weather," he said. "Otherwise, I cannot be held responsible for the consequences."

He commissioned Chaplain George Metcalf to write the following prayer, which he had printed on three hundred thousand Christmas cards:

> Almighty and most merciful Father, we humbly beseech thee, of thy great goodness, to restrain these immoderate rains with which we have had to contend. Grant us fair weather for battle. Graciously hearken to us as soldiers who call upon thee that armed with thy power, we may advance from victory to victory, and crush the oppression and wickedness of our enemies, and establish thy justice among men and nations. Amen.[5]

It worked. The skies broke, the Allied air force went to work, and the German offensive was repulsed. Patton thanked the Lord in front of his staff. Four days later, the skies clouded up again.[6]

The Gulf War of 1991 provides a more recent example of divine intervention, provoked once again by a praying general.

Operation Desert Storm might not have gone so well had it not been for the amazing wind shift that occurred fifteen minutes before the ground attack began at 4:00 a.m. on February 24. According to marine Major General Charles Krulak, the wind always blows in the same direction in that part of the world. But during the attack, it reversed direction and blew in favor of the Allied forces, from southwest to northeast. This neutralized the threat of poison gas, because the wind would have blown the gas back toward the Iraqis. Within a few minutes after cease-fire orders were issued on February 28, the wind resumed its normal course.

Scripture says, "He makes his angels winds, his servants flames of fire" (Hebrews 1:7). General Krulak attributes the miracle to prayer.[7]

Frequently God's angelic warriors are seen, not by those whom they are protecting, but by their enemies. How often missionaries have been protected by a contingent of heavenly honor guards.

It happened in 1956 during the Mau Mau uprisings in East Africa. The story is told by Morris Plotts. A band of roving Mau Maus came to the village of Lauri, surrounded it, and killed every one of the three hundred inhabitants, including women and children.

Not more than three miles away was the Rift Valley School, a private boarding school for children of missionaries. Immediately upon leaving the carnage of Lauri, the Mau Maus came with spears, bows and arrows, clubs, and torches to the school.

Of course, you can imagine the fear of the children along with their instructors housed in the boarding school. Word had already reached them about the destruction of Lauri. Since flight seemed impossible, the faculty united in fervent prayer.

Out of the darkness of the night, lighted torches were seen coming toward the school. Soon there was a complete ring of terrorists about the school, cutting off all avenues of escape. Shouting and curses could be heard.

The Mau Maus began to advance on the school, tightening the circle, shouting louder, coming closer. All of a sudden, when they got close enough to throw a spear . . . they stopped. They began to retreat and soon were running into the jungle.

A call had gone out to the authorities, and an army unit had been sent in the direction of the school to attempt to rescue the inhabitants. By the time the army arrived, the attackers had dispersed. The army searched for and managed to capture the entire band of raiding Mau Maus.

Later, the judge at their trial questioned the leader: "On this particular night, did you kill the inhabitants of Lauri?"

"Yes."

"Was it your intent to do the same at the school in Rift Valley?"

"Yes."

"Well, then," asked the judge, "why did you not complete the mission? Why didn't you attack the school?"

The leader of the Mau Maus said: "We were on our way to attack and destroy all the people and school, but as we came closer, all of a sudden, between us and the school there were many huge men, dressed in white with flaming swords, and we became afraid and ran to hide!"

The angel of the Lord still encamps around those who fear Him and delivers them (see Psalm 34:7).

Booton Herndon, in his book *The Seventh Day*,[8] tells the story of Faole, a native of Papua, who killed his first man at the age of fifteen, then went on to kill three more, two women and a child, simply for the joy of killing. Later, the law caught up with him, and he went to jail. After he was released, Faole appeared at a little Christian mission run by the Seventh-day Adventists and requested permission to go to school. Faole would not take No for an answer.

Soon Faole, the most feared man in the district, became the most respected. When a new mission was opened, and the missionary was authorized to take an assistant with him, he chose Faole. Finally Faole was given a position as teacher on his own in the village of Maibikee. The bush people learned to love him. He built a new village, clean and neat. A fine church was erected, attendance at the school grew, and the village prospered.

But at the nearest village, a few miles over the mountain, the natives continued their evil ways. They grew suspicious of what was happening at Maibikee, and when their chief suddenly died one day, the medicine man announced that a spell had been put upon him by the people of Maibikee. It would be necessary to destroy Maibikee, burn it to the ground, and kill all its people. That night, fifty warriors in full war paint, with arrows and sharpened spears, set out to accomplish the mission.

One defector in the village traveled for two days to alert the missionary, who set out immediately for Maibikee. There, two days later, the perspiring missionary was pleased and surprised to find the village in perfect order and Faole himself fit as a fiddle. It turned out that Faole had sensed something in the air that night and had gathered his family around him for prayers. He had picked up the Bible and opened it haphazardly, and his eyes had fallen upon the Thirty-fourth Psalm, in which was written: "The angel of the Lord encamps around those who fear him, and he delivers them."

Faole had promptly stopped worrying and had gone to bed and slept soundly.

But what had happened to the warriors? The missionary set out for the village over the hill. There he found things in a most unsettled condition. The men seemed sullen, the women mocking. The missionary asked the headman where he had been four nights before. The headman at first refused to answer, then finally admitted that he and his warriors had started out for Maibikee to kill Faole.

Why hadn't he? The headman was furious. "You know, all right!" he said. "Because when we got there, you and a whole group of white men, all dressed in white, stood in a ring around Faole's house and remained there all night!"

The painted warriors hid in the bush until dawn, then slunk away home.

We could include another dozen such stories in this chapter, but instead, let's discuss an interesting question. What is the greatest miracle in this story: the angelic guardians or the change in Faole's life from evil to goodness?

What is the greatest of miracles? Is it to create a star? This God we serve hurls galaxies into space and then places huge black holes in the middle of them that suck in everything around them, even light. We don't know why. But that's not hard for Him. And to make a mere planet; why, that's nothing. When God created this planet, every atom leapt up to do His will; every molecule formed a perfect unity and took its assigned place in the grand scheme of life. He speaks, and the light breaks forth; the darkness flees. Every branch waves His praises. Every clump of dirt obeys the laws of physics laid down for it.

Ah, but what happens when He seeks to recreate a heart? When God speaks to that stronghold of the enemy, there is a dark force that resists His will, a shrinking back, a turning away. Only the sinful heart naturally refuses the voice of its Maker.

So the greatest miracle of all is when that heart responds to the call of grace and submits to the scalpel of the Master Physician and is made new. The most incredible miracle is not when the physically sick are made whole but when a liar is made true, an arrogant person is made humble, a cruel person becomes kind. Such miracles happen every day. They can happen to anyone who surrenders to the Captain of the hosts.

Angels are fighting over you. You may think that in this titanic struggle between the forces of good and evil, your part is insignificant. Oh no! Worlds are watching you. Invisible majesties wait with baited breath to see what choices you will make. Someday, millions of years hence, you might be serving God as the ruler of galaxies, clothed in inconceivable splendor. Or your name may be just a dark memory. Everything you do advances the kingdom of light or the kingdom of darkness. Every prayer is a blow against the forces of evil, while every self-indulgence, every sin of greed or anger, is a triumph for the enemy. Your cowardice may cause many to fall; or your bravery, your persistence in prayer, may start a ripple that turns back tides of evil. Your self-denial may set into action forces for good that will resound throughout eternity; your loving deeds may be enshrined with immortal honors that you cannot now conceive. You are not alone. All of the forces of heaven are waiting to come to your aid, as they did for Daniel.

Most of the local skirmishes in this struggle between good and evil are fought on the invisible battleground of the heart. But there remains one last great battle before evil is vanquished. The next time God marshals His angelic army in full force, at His second coming, will mark the end of this world as we know it. The Apocalypse describes this next great battle on God's celestial timetable:

> I saw heaven standing open and there before me was a white horse, whose rider is called Faithful and True. With justice he judges and makes war. His eyes are like blazing fire, and on his head are many crowns. . . . The armies of heaven were following him, riding on white horses and dressed in fine linen, white and clean. . . . Then I saw the beast and the kings of the earth and their armies gathered together to make war against the rider on the horse and his army (Revelation 19:11-19).

The outcome of this great battle-to-end-all-battles is not in doubt; those who are fighting God will face a horrible punishment:

> The cowardly, the unbelieving, the vile, the murderers, the sexually immoral, those who practice magic arts, the idolaters and all liars—their place will be in the fiery lake of burning sulfur. This is the second death (Revelation 21:8).

When Jesus comes "in his Father's glory with his angels, . . . he will reward each person according to what he has done" (Matthew 16:27). The angels, who in the past have so often shielded God's people from harm and been agents of mercy, will then be agents of destruction to the wicked:

> The Son of Man will send out his angels, and they will
> weed out of his kingdom everything that causes sin and all
> who do evil. They will throw them into the fiery furnace,
> where there will be weeping and gnashing of teeth (Mat-
> thew 13:41, 42; see also Jude14, 15; Matthew 24:30, 31;
> 2 Thessalonians 1:7, 8).

God does not inflict such horrible retribution without warning.
According to Revelation 14, shortly before the end of time, God sends
three special angels to earth with a message about judgment to come.
These angels warn all who refuse to worship the Maker of heaven and
earth of the tragic destiny they have chosen. This is no arbitrary, self-
serving decree on God's part. All who refuse to worship God eventually end up worshiping self or another self worshiper. But self-
worship is toxic to the cosmos, with ultimate results similar to the
holocaust of Hitler's Germany or Pol Pot's Cambodia. That is, given
time, opportunity, and unlimited power, self-worship produces a
Nero, a Stalin, a devil. The only thing a merciful God can do is to
surgically remove this cancer from the universe.

The everlasting gospel is a terrible thing to spurn.

And what is the everlasting gospel?

When the Son of God came to this earth two thousand years
ago—the mission was too important to entrust to an angel—He was
arrested under trumped-up charges and condemned to death. At
that time, His disciples made a feeble attempt to defend Him with
the sword. Jesus rebuked their well-meaning but misguided efforts: "Do you think I cannot call on my Father, and he will at once
put at my disposal more than twelve legions of angels?" (Matthew
26:53)—that is, a legion for each of the disciples.

But that wasn't the plan. As Jesus hung on the cross, all the armies
of heaven were at His disposal. But the One whom every angel in
heaven longed—yearned—to deliver refused their help and embraced
a shameful death. By His torment, He purchased our bliss and opened
heaven to all who accept Him as Lord and Saviour.

111

IN THE PRESENCE OF ANGELS

On the cross, Jesus won the battle between the forces of good and evil for us. He conquered by the startling strategy of surrender. His sacrifice opened the floodgates of divine mercy and power, and that mighty cataract of grace is still flowing, offering pardon for the past and a new beginning.

But not for long. The window of grace is destined to close. Today, He woos, He warns; tomorrow, He wages war. The next time Jesus comes, it will not be as a humble carpenter but as a conquering king, leading the armies of heaven in the final showdown with evil. You can't avoid the battle; you must choose one side or the other. Confronted with overwhelming force, you, too, can conquer only by surrender. Your best bet is to surrender to the One to whom has been given all power in heaven and earth, who is coming again soon to take His children home.

> May he strengthen your hearts so that you will be blameless and holy in the presence of our God and Father when our Lord Jesus comes with all his holy ones (1 Thessalonians 3:13).

---

1. William H. Shea, "Wrestling with the prince of Persia: A study on Daniel 10," *Andrews University Seminary Studies*, 21:3 (Autumn 1983), 225-250. I have not followed Dr. Shea in identifying the "prince of Persia" with a historical human being, as his position is not supported by scholarly consensus.

2. C. Peter Wagner and F. Douglas Pennoyer, eds., *Wrestling With Dark Angels* (Ventura: Regal Books, 1990).

3. *Strange Stories, Amazing Facts* (Pleasantville, N.Y.: The Reader's Digest Association, 1976), 376; H. C. Moolenburgh, *Meetings With Angels* (Saffron Walden, Essex, England: C. W. Daniel Company, 1992), 144f.

4. H. C. Moolenburgh, *Meetings With Angels*, translated from the Dutch by Tony Langham and Pym Peters (Great Britain: C. W. Daniel, 1992),146-148.

5. George Metcalf, "Prayer for Fair Weather," *Guideposts*, December 1994.

6. H. C. Moolenburgh, *A Handbook of Angels*, translated from the Dutch by Amina Marix-Evans (Great Britain: C. W. Daniel Co., 1988), 204.

7. Carey Kinsolving, "Miracle Well," *World*, 29 August 1992, 21.

8. (New York: McGraw-Hill, 1960), 165f.

CHAPTER

8

Deliver Us From Evil

It was nearly sundown as two men walked quickly along the dusty road. Intent on their mission, they ignored the stares of the curious villagers. Shepherds could be seen leading their flocks to the safety of their folds for the approaching night. Along the road were vineyards, their well-tended grapevines heavy with ripening fruit. Graceful date palms waved in the gentle evening breeze near the city wall. It was a scene of luxurious prosperity, with no hint of impending doom.

Lot, Abraham's nephew, happened to be sitting near

113

the town gate when the two strangers approached. He got up to meet them, suspecting that the travelers had no accommodations for the night. He greeted them with the customary bow and invited them to enjoy the hospitality of his own home. They courteously declined, but Lot pressed the invitation.

Sodom was a dangerous place for strangers to sleep at night. Lot finally persuaded the two travelers to come home with him. He fed them a good meal and made them comfortable. Genesis 19:4, 5 tells us what happened next.

> Before they had gone to bed, all the men from every part of the city of Sodom—both young and old—surrounded the house. They called to Lot, "Where are the men who came to you tonight? Bring them out to us so that we can have sex with them."

Lot decided he'd better step outside and calm his lust-crazed neighbors and make an effort to persuade them to leave his two guests alone, but his words were like pouring gasoline on fire. They threatened Lot and rushed toward the door. At that point, his two houseguests—who were really angels—pulled him back into the house and struck his antagonists blind.

Some people can't seem to take a hint. Lot's neighbors kept searching for the door of his house, even after the two angels had supernaturally blinded them.

The angels told Lot that they were going to destroy the city because of its great wickedness. So Lot hurried out to tell his daughters and sons-in-law, but they didn't take him seriously. Even Lot seemed reluctant to leave Sodom, so the angels finally took him, his wife, and their two unmarried daughters by their hands and brought them out of Sodom—just ahead of the devouring flames. That day, Sodom was destroyed by fire.

God protects His own. That protection does not usually extend to destroying the wicked—not yet. Only rarely does God choose to unleash the forces of nature upon evil cities as He did at Sodom. But it does still happen.

Consider what happened to the lovely, flourishing city of Messina, Italy, in 1908. In the early morning of December 28, an earthquake struck, with devastating loss of life. A few hours earlier, some of the wicked inhabitants had passed a series of violent resolutions.

Every city has wicked people in it, but in this case, the city leaders officially voted against God. The journal *Il Telefono*, printed in Messina, published in its Christmas issue an abominable parody, daring the Almighty to make Himself known by sending an earthquake! Three days later, the earthquake came.[1]

According to *Encyclopaedia Britannica*, 160,000 people died in this quake. Some authorities say 120,000. This is the largest known death toll of any earthquake that has ever occurred in a Christian nation. Perhaps, as in Sodom, God could not find even a handful of righteous people in the city.

Usually God doesn't intervene on such a massive scale. But one of the reasons He sends angels to this earth is to protect His children from evil people. Sometimes He uses angels in human form; sometimes He uses mysterious knocks on the door; sometimes He even uses animals, like white dogs and green lizards. Creative, isn't He?

The motel where my sisters and I had made reservations to stay in the town of Yulee, Florida, was in a very out-of-the-way place. Instead of rooms, it had cabins set way back from the highway. I had an uneasy feeling about the place, but we had already taken care of our luggage, and my sisters were lying on the bed, resting. It had been a long day, and all we wanted to do was to stretch out and relax. Soon, however, we heard a lot of cussing and swearing coming from the other side of the duplex cabin. There was a door going from our side of the cabin to the other, with only a slide lock on the door. We could not hear every word being said, but we heard enough to know the man was talking about us!

When we had first arrived, a car had been parked on our side of the cabin, and my sister Arlene had gone to knock on the door to ask the man to please move his car out of our way. He had been sleeping and was wearing only his under garments when he came to the door, cussing and swearing at her. He got dressed and moved the automobile. Arlene noticed a pistol on his night stand and mentioned it to us, but she still felt as if we would be safe enough with the doors locked and my two dogs for protection.

I didn't share her feelings and was very sure we could be murdered if we didn't get out immediately. I tried to talk both of my sisters into packing up and getting out of there, but they just didn't seem to want to be bothered at eleven o'clock at night. I started to pray for something to happen to change their minds. Suddenly I heard both of them scream at the top of their lungs. I looked and saw something green in the middle of their bed! A lizard had jumped from the windowsill onto the bed, leaping right between them.

I laughed and said, "Well, are you ready to get out of here yet?"

"Yes!" they said. We packed up and were out of there in twenty minutes.

We went about ten miles down the road and rented another room at a motel that looked like it was safe. As we were registering at the desk, the woman said to us, "At a motel about ten miles down the road, there have been several unsolved murders committed in the last few months." When she mentioned the name of the place, it was the same name as the motel we had just left! We all got goose bumps, and I thank the Lord for sending the lizard to drive my sisters out of there.

-Imelda M., Harrison, Maine

Roneide de Oliveira is the wife of Tiago ("James" in English), who translated for Tim when he conducted meetings in southern Brazil. Before Roneide and Tiago were married, she was studying theology in São Paulo at the Instituto Adventista de Ensino (IAE). She was staying at her aunt's house an hour away from the college in the barrio of Moema.

During this period, she had been spending half an hour a day in prayer. Her aunt used to say, "Why do you spend so much time kneeling and praying? Do you think you're going to get everything in life just by praying?"

"It's not enough to stay there praying; you also have to do something," Roneide replied.

Now Moema was a very rich barrio, but it was also very dangerous, with many nightclubs that catered to perversion. Roneide had previously gotten a ride at night with a classmate, but he had become so frightened that he refused to take her home anymore.

One night after attending a Week of Prayer program, she took a bus from the college back to her aunt's house. She stepped off the bus late at night to climb the seven blocks to her home, praying all the while for protection.

While concentrating on her praying, she did not at first realize that she was being followed by a large, dark green car. When she was on the next-to-the-last block, she noticed the car. She decided she would not look but keep her eyes downward on the road, hiding her face.

Suddenly she felt the presence of something soft and fluffy that touched her legs at about knee level. It was an extremely white dog. It seemed to have come out of nowhere. The dog stayed beside her all the way. Because Moema is a rich barrio, no dogs run loose in that neighborhood. A few of the rich people do own a certain breed of dog, but this dog was not that breed.

117

IN THE PRESENCE OF ANGELS

The car went to the end of the road, turned around, and was coming back toward her as she approached her aunt's gate. Thinking whoever was in the car was going to open the door and grab her, she quickened her pace. The dog did likewise. Finally, the car turned away and went down the road. Roneide ran across the road to the gate. When she turned to look back at the dog, it was gone.

When the dog left, she felt extremely vulnerable. The corner where her aunt lived was a particularly dangerous one, and before she could go inside, she had to press the bell and wait for someone to open the door, come outside, and open the gate. When her aunt finally came to the door, she said, "Are you crazy? You could have been killed."

"Yes, I know," replied Roneide, "but I do trust in the protecting power of God."

Patricia T., of Pierceton, Indiana, met her angel during World War II. Patricia had moved to Beaufort, South Carolina, so she could be near her sailor husband Robert, who was stationed at Parris Island Marine Base, a boot camp for marines. She frequently traveled the thirty miles by bus to the base to visit her husband.

One evening Patricia stayed with her husband later than usual and ended up taking the last seat on the last bus back to Beaufort. During the half-hour ride back, she found herself thinking about the bodies of two young girls that had been found in the nearby swamp the previous month. The murders were unsolved. As she glanced over her shoulder, she noticed the dark eyes of a sailor fixed on her. Nervous and apprehensive, she began to dread the dark walk home.

Finally the bus stopped at the little shack that served as a depot. It had one bare light bulb in front of the door. Patricia prayed as she stepped off the bus. Her apartment was five blocks away on the main street; all was dark in between. Patricia writes:

I walked away from the bus as rapidly as possible, hearing the chatter and laughter of the crowd drift away. I sensed the presence of someone following me. As in a nightmare, the steps kept drawing closer. At the end of the second block, the dark-haired sailor caught up with me.

The street was deserted. To the left was a large wooden fence; to the right, the dirt merged with fields of swamp grass. Terrified, I glanced up to the far end of the road ,where one street light shone faintly. The stranger, without a word, put his arm around me and started to pull me toward the fence. I struggled to stay on the path, talking to him quietly, asking him to leave me alone, assuring him that he didn't want to do this. Meanwhile, under my breath, I was praying the whole time.

Looking toward the far street lamp, I thought, *Oh, if only I could get to that corner.* I then noticed that the light appeared to become brighter. I made a sudden jerk, and my struggle with the man began in earnest. Desperately looking for any help from anywhere, my head turned to the street light again. There, in the glow of the light, stood a tall, imposing MP—a military policeman—clad in khaki. I told the sailor to leave me alone, or I would scream for that MP over there.

Suddenly a thought flashed into my mind: where did that MP come from? The sailor dropped his arms hastily, and we walked in silence to the end of the street. I never took my eyes off the MP or the light.

At the corner, the sailor turned to the left, and I to the right. He flung a parting shot, yelling, "I'll see YOU again!" The MP never glanced at the sailor; his eyes followed me as I moved up the half block to my apartment.

Now that the danger was over, I kept thinking how strange the sudden appearance of this MP was. I opened the screen door and turned around for one last look at him. His eyes were still riveted on me. Dashing up the stairs to the window facing the street, I pressed against the screen to see my "savior" once more.

He was gone! No one was there! Incredulously, my eyes searched the whole long street for him; I ran back downstairs to look out from the screen door but saw no one. Could a jeep have taken him away? The only sound came from the tree frogs and cicadas.

Turning slowly, I moved up the stairs and back to the window, my mind in a whirl. Was it my imagination? No! The sailor saw him. My knees still shook from the terror of the encounter. There on the windowsill, looking out into the darkness, I didn't feel like a brave eighteen-year-old bride anymore, just a scared little girl. The tears began to fall as I asked, "Lord, what happened?"

The full significance of this experience did not hit me until about fifteen years later as I struggled with another destroyer. My life consisted of black, miserable days and nights. I doubted, at that time, all the values that had previously sustained me. I could not believe God was real. If God did exist, I thought, why had such terrible things happened to destroy my life ?

One day, as I sank into the pit of despondency, I called, perhaps for the last time, "God help me; are You there? Do You save?" As I seemed to sink into a dark void, a light appeared in my memory. It seemed as real as the wet pillow under my face. Suddenly, once again, I saw the black night, the dirt path; I felt the pull on my shoulders. And then I saw again the street in Beaufort, the MP, the light glowing behind him as he watched me, never taking his eyes from my face.

Looking down through the years, God knew I would have this terrible time in my life and would need to know His saving power. Once more, I needed an angel to save me. My tears flowed—and still come—as I thank God for saving my body and my soul. From that day to this, when doubts arise (and the accuser of the brethren still puts them there), I remember the time I saw my angel, and the shadows flee.

Sometimes young women find themselves in need of a big brother to protect them. Andrea S. discovered she had a big brother she didn't know about. I (Tim) heard the story directly from her own lips.

Andrea, age eighteen, was a student at the Instituto Adventista Cruzeiro do Sul (IACS) in south Brazil. One Tuesday morning in 1993, she said her usual prayer for protection. That evening, after attending a choir rehearsal at the school, she set out on foot for home, which was just over one-half mile away. When she got close to the last turn before her house, a car stopped beside her, and the male driver commanded her to "step inside here because I want to take you with me."

"I'm not going with you," Andrea replied, and kept on walking.

At this, the driver flew into a rage and pointed a gun at Andrea, so she stopped. As he was opening the door to step out of the car, a tall young man suddenly stepped up and stood beside her. He was blond, and his looks were very unusual, to say the least.

"What do you want with my sister?" he said.

Andrea's assailant replied, "You'd better shut up; otherwise, I'll kill you both."

"You can kill us both," replied the mysterious blonde, "but you will have to suffer the consequences, because you are alone against all the rest of us." And he gestured toward someone or something that Andrea could not see.

Andrea's would-be attacker looked in the direction indicated and saw something that terrified him. He blanched, jumped into the car, revved the engine, and spun away as fast as possible.

The blond man touched her shoulder and told Andrea that she

could now cross the road because the danger had passed.

When she had crossed the road, her real brother, age fifteen, was coming to meet her. When she turned back to the man who had helped her, he had vanished.

This story might be entitled "The Summer of '42," since that's when it happened. Mary Futcher, who now lives in Hawaii, is a close personal friend of the Melashenko family. In 1942 she was giving Bible studies in New York. At the end of one particularly tiring day, she arrived at her last appointment of the evening at 6:30 p.m. in Brooklyn. Several people were in attendance, and their many questions caused the session to last until 11:30 p.m.

Mary faced an hour's ride on the subway to get to her apartment on West Riverside, a few blocks from her church. She had two choices: the faster Independent subway or the slower I. R. T. The I. R. T. would take her to within one block of her home, but the Independent would force her to walk several blocks through Harlem.

Since it was a clear, beautiful evening, she decided on the faster Independent subway, hoping to be home and in bed sooner.

Well, when I got off the subway, I began to walk hurriedly because the street was dark. As I walked along, I thought of the decisions the young people in my Bible study had made to accept Jesus. I was thrilled.

All of a sudden, a big hand pulled me in between two buildings. Fear crept over me, and a numbness I had never felt before struck me from head to toe. All I could do was cling to my purse with my Bible inside. I uttered inwardly, "Oh, God, help me!"

Just as I uttered those words inaudibly, the hand that had grabbed me let me go. I fell over like a sack of potatoes. My assailant screamed as he ran out from between the buildings, directly into a policeman. By this time I had picked myself up and walked out to the street. My attacker was a huge man, about six-foot-two. He told the policeman that a bolt of lightning had struck him, which made him let go of me. I explained to both of them that I was a Christian and on my way home from a Bible study. The policeman asked if I wanted to press charges, but my attacker promised never to do such a thing again, so I gave him some literature and prayed for him.

The policeman, never asking me where I lived, said he would walk me home. In my confusion, I never asked his name, but as he walked me home, he explained to me the dangers of walking in that neighborhood alone at such a late hour. He was so very kind and pleasant, both in the way he talked to me and in the way he handled my attacker.

He led me right to my door and opened the outside apartment door for me. When I turned around to thank this kind policeman, he was nowhere in sight.

After I got into my apartment, I got on my knees and thanked Jesus for saving me that night and for sending my protecting angel to help me. A call to the police station the next morning confirmed that this policeman was indeed an angel. No one knew of any policeman walking that particular beat that night.

On February 13, 1983, Debra S., of Camas, Washington, was washing clothes in the laundry room of her apartment complex, when she was confronted by a man wearing a black ski mask and pointing a gun at her head.

I really thought it was a joke and asked him, "Are you kidding? Is this for real?"

His reply was a vicious "Shut up, shut up!" At that point, I lifted up my head and silently prayed, "Dear God and Jesus, please help me." Suddenly I remembered the Mace on my key chain, but a thought came to me—*not yet*.

We heard sirens in the distance, and he seemed to panic and repeated in the same vicious voice, "Shut up. Listen, I think that's for me." . . .

I realized he was serious. Feeling stunned, I turned around. He had a funny look in his eyes, and he put his right hand on my shoulder, propelling me toward the back door. After he got me out the back door, he put a knife to my throat. I was in shock. He told me that if I screamed, he would cut me.

He put his hand over my mouth, and I felt like I was going to suffocate. Then he took me a few steps from the door and started to take me toward the back left side of the building.

The feeling of cold death overcame me. My voice changed to a child's as I pleaded, "Please don't take me back there. I'm scared of the dark." He stopped for a second, then turned me back in the other direction, still with the knife at my throat. Then he put his ski mask on my head backward.

I felt his hand moving behind me, fumbling with something as if undoing his pants. He again told me not to scream. He still had the knife against my throat with my right arm pinned so that I was only able to move my right hand.

Suddenly I thought of the Mace again. Very, very carefully I slipped my hand into the right front pocket of my sweater, put my hand on the leather cover to the Mace, and turned the nozzle to be able to spray him.

I got a good grip on the Mace, making sure the key ring that was attached didn't make any noise.

With all my strength, I tore my arm from his grip ,at the same time screaming and spraying the Mace at him behind me over my left shoulder. He knocked me to the ground, telling me to quit screaming or he would stuff a sock in my mouth.

His hand covered my mouth as he was sitting on top of me, so

I bit him. Not wanting to seriously hurt him, I loosened my bite, but then he started beating me in the head. I knew that if I didn't do something quickly, he would knock me out.

From somewhere, I got a surge of strength. Arching my body, I threw him some distance into the bushes.

As I got up to my knees, I saw a peaceful, soft light glowing through the branches of the trees. I felt a presence. I put my hand toward the light. My hand was taken by the hand of an angel. The angel lifted me to my feet.

I felt a powerful feeling of truth and life, of justice. It was an almost indescribable feeling.

Something told me, "Step out of your slippers." As I stepped out of my slippers, the angel's hand pulled me, then yanked me and let go fast, as if to tell me to run.

I hadn't run far when I slowed down, thinking my attacker probably wasn't chasing me anymore. But when I looked back, he was close behind me. I sped up, but slipped and fell. He fell right behind me.

He told me to stop as I was crawling away. I sensed by his voice that he felt truly sorry.

All of a sudden, the word *no* flashed into my head as if the angel was telling me, "No! Don't trust him."

I got up and continued running around a corner. When I rounded the next corner, I came face to face with the assistant manager, whose wife had heard my screams. I was hysterical by this time, so I screamed when I saw him. I was such an apparition by this time that he screamed in shock and surprise.

I was covered in mud; my hair was wet. I had blood coming from my mouth. My sweater was inside out. But most of all, I think it was my terror that conveyed itself and caused him to scream, because he wasn't the type who got scared easily.

The police were called, but they were unable to catch the villain. Debra had been studying various religions, but after the attack, she became depressed and didn't pursue any kind of religion. But God was working with her.

In the past year I've become a born-again Christian, and now I have a very fruitful and personal relationship with Christ.

I'm a wife and mother of three children. All I can say is thank God for His mercy and His ability to hear our prayers and to oftentimes save our lives through His miracles.

Normally, angels are minimalists—they get the job done with the least possible interference in earthly affairs. In the preceding story, Debra's angel might have prevented the attack altogether. But then Debra would never have known of God's intervention in her life. Instead, the angel provided her with just enough aid to sustain her through the trial and to prevent further tragedy.

Sometimes the intervention is even more minimal—nothing more than a knock at the door, as in the following two stories.

Before Mother married my father, he took her to some square dances. There, she met a young ruffian who decided that he wanted to make her his wife. She informed him politely that she was going to marry my father. At that, he flew into a rage and swore he would kill her before he would let her marry anyone but himself.

Well, Mother married Father in 1905, and they went to live in the house he had built on top of a hill. One morning, Father made Mother stay in bed because she had a fever. He had to take a wagonload of wheat to a man living several miles away.

Soon after he left, there was loud knocking on the door. Thinking it was a neighbor, Mother called out, "Come in!" but the knocking only continued. Finally, she arose, donned her robe, and went to the door. No one was there. After checking all the windows and doors, she returned to bed.

Immediately, the knocking started again. This time she hurried back to the door. Again, nobody was there, but upon looking down the hill, she saw the man who had threatened to kill her coming up with a gun over his shoulder.

Quickly, she locked the door and hastened to lock the other door and windows, pulling down all the shades. Then, exhausted, she fell into bed.

Soon she heard loud pounding and kicking on the doors, then shouting outside every window, "I know you're in there! I saw Bob leave a while ago. Let me in!"

Mother cowered under the covers, weeping and praying for protection.

At last, the terrible sounds stopped. She was still in bed, trembling, when Father came home. Amazed to find everything locked (people rarely locked their doors back then), he knocked and knocked. When his wife did not come to the door, he went to the bedroom window and called her name. Only then did Mother let Father in. She then fell into his arms, sobbing out the story.

When the tears were finally dried, Father asked, "But who knocked on the door in the first place, warning you?" They could only deduce that an angel had warned Mother.

—Mrs. Stephen B., Riverside, California.

Being a fairly new Christian, I am only now learning to believe in angels. After remembering something that happened to me, I realized that angels had saved my life.

I lived in Nashville, Tennessee, when I was in my early twenties. I stayed with my sister while working at a Laundromat.

While talking with some customers doing laundry, I happened to mention to two young men that I was looking for a room to rent. They said that they owned a mobile home in a lot not far away and would be willing to rent it to me for a good price.

I didn't own a car at that time, so they offered to drive me there. I stopped by my sister's home and explained where I was going with them and told her that I would be home later.

They took me to a deserted-looking mobile home park with a few homes spread quite far apart. Once I stepped into the home to look around, one of the men took out a knife and told me we were going to have a little "fun." I tried to get away from them, but they kept trying to force me onto the bed. Needless to say, I was scared to death. Then there was a loud knock on the door.

The one man held me down while the other answered the door. There was no one there. He stepped outside and looked around but still could not see anyone.

He came back and again tried to hold me down on the bed. Once again, there was a loud knock on the door. The one man ran to answer it and ran around the home, but no one was there.

No sooner had he gotten back inside than the knocking started again. He looked at his friend and said, "This is too weird—let's get out of here!" and they took off.

After looking around outside, I couldn't figure out how anyone could have knocked on the door and gotten away without being seen. I always wondered about this and have told the story to several of my friends, who have also wondered. Now I realize that it was my guardian angel there to save me.

—Nancy B., Anaheim, California.

Finally, here are two stories involving people in automobiles who found themselves on the wrong side of the tracks.

John M., of LaSalle, Colorado, is a minister. He and I (Lonnie) were fellow Seminary students at Andrews University from 1968 to 1970. In September of 1969, he and his wife were returning to the Seminary from Brunswick, Maine. On the way, they spent a day at EXPO '67 in Montreal, Canada, leaving the fair at about 8:00 p.m.

It was a hot, sultry summer day, and at the time, tension between the French and the English was running high. Somehow John and his wife got lost and ended up in a very rough part of town. They felt very conspicuous—an apparently rich American couple driving a nearly new Ford LTD in a poor section of Montreal. The streets were full of youth trying to escape the unbearable heat in their apartments. A crowd of young men began moving in around the couple, slowing them down. John and his wife locked the doors, prayed, and tried to keep going.

All of a sudden, as if from nowhere, a big dump truck appeared and pulled ahead of them on the right. The driver shouted, "You lost? Follow me!" The crowd parted for the big truck, and the Martins followed not more than one foot from his tailgate. The truck led them through several streets before coming to an entrance ramp. The driver leaned out of his window, pointed up the ramp, and shouted, "U.S.A. that way." They sped past him, then turned to wave thanks; but the truck and driver had disappeared.

John and his wife believe God sent an angel in a dump truck to save them.

Ivadell E., of Sumas, Washington, sent us this story about David G., who lives in Lima, Peru. It is 19.5 miles from David's home to his office. There are two ways to get to work: a longer, safer way, which he takes when he has women or children with him, and a shorter, more dangerous way, through the Peligroso district.

129

IN THE PRESENCE OF ANGELS

One day David was traveling home alone from his office with a car full of computers, and he took the shortcut through the rough section of town. At the worst possible time, his car broke down.

The car would not budge. Two men started in his direction. They seemed to have an eye on the computers.

Suddenly, another "man" appeared, a man with a perfect face. David stared at his face because it was so different from the hardened faces he usually saw in this area. The face of this stranger was so perfect that he looked like a movie star. David was so captivated by him that he forgot all about his predicament.

The stranger approached him, saying, "You must get out of here. These men are going to accost you. They have already finished with one victim."

With that, the man with the beautiful face pushed David's car and . . . it just went!

David is sure it was an angel who saved him. Perhaps he was familiar with the words of another David, in Psalm 35:

> May those who seek my life be disgraced and put to shame; may those who plot my ruin be turned back in dismay. May they be like chaff before the wind, with the angel of the Lord driving them away. . . . Then my soul will rejoice in the Lord and delight in his salvation. My whole being will exclaim, "Who is like you, O LORD? You rescue the poor from those too strong for them, the poor and needy from those who rob them."

---

1. John Lawrence, *Down to Earth* (Wheaton, Ill.: Tyndale, 1983), 51.

CHAPTER

9

In the Presence of Danger

This incident happened many years ago when my daughter Eileen was eleven (she's now in her early forties) and I was in my mid-thirties. It was summertime, and my Uncle Smithy took my son (fifteen), my daughter, and me to Huntington Beach, California, to swim. Eileen and I went in the water together, but my son and my uncle stayed on the beach.

The water was warm, and we were enjoying our time together until we suddenly found ourselves being swept out to sea by a tremendous undertow. Soon we were out of our depth and being swept toward the cement pilings of the Huntington Beach pier! I told my daughter to hang on to me while I bounced up and down, trying to keep us afloat.

Being a Christian, I prayed all the time I was bobbing up and down, "Please, dear Lord, if You can send help, thank You. If not, we give ourselves over to You in death until Jesus comes, if this is the way we're going to die!"

I realized my energy was quickly being drained and that I wouldn't have the strength to keep bouncing up and down, especially with my daughter's weight on me. I reached the point of my last ounce of ability to keep from drowning.

At the moment of my last "bounce" and my last cry for help (though no swimmers were near us, nor did anyone hear us), we heard a voice in the ocean call to us. A woman swam to us, saying, "Hang on to me and have your daughter hang on to you, and I will swim you to safety!" She swam with such tremendous strength that it felt as if we were flying through the water. In no time at all, we were standing on the shore safe and sound. We turned around in our dazed condition to say "thank you," but no one was there on the shore or in the water anywhere near us!

My daughter Eileen said, "Mother, that must have been an angel who saved our lives!"

I said, "You're right. Jesus heard our prayers and knew we had no other help."

When we told my son and uncle what had happened, we all agreed it was a miracle of God, and we had the awesome privilege of seeing an angel face to face! Truly, God is love!

—Eloise T., North Hollywood, California

The stories in this chapter continue the theme of deliverance from evil, but the evil is impersonal; the danger is from nature or circumstances rather than evil men. Here are several more stories of people who were delivered from the sea.

Thank you for this opportunity to share my experience with you regarding an angel. Though it happened many years ago, I remember it in complete detail. From childhood, I had been taught about Jesus and His love for us, but this happening was not just a story or imagining—it was real and confirmed His existence, His presence, and His miracles to me.

In the early fifties my husband and I decided to take our two young sons (ages two and four) to the Atlantic seashore for a vacation. We rented a cottage in the middle of nowhere—no other cottages, stores, or traffic—just miles and miles of beautiful white beach as far as the eye could see. Lots of sand and crabs. We had a wonderful time, and though the boys loved the beach, we parents didn't take our eyes off them for a moment.

About the third day, when the children awoke just after sunrise, I told my husband to stay in bed and I would amuse the boys so he could get a little more rest. We put on our bathing suits, gathered the toys, and headed for the beach.

As we came over the hill, we saw that the water was rough and the waves were crashing on the sand. The elder boy started screaming with fright, so I leaned over to tell him to just sit down and play with his cars. And as I stood up and looked all around, I discovered that my younger son had disappeared. I knew there was only one place to look, but I dreaded what I might see.

Suddenly I heard running footsteps behind me, and a man in a swimsuit swept past me and dashed out into the waves. He plucked the child from danger, brought him to me, and laid him in my arms without saying a word. When I looked up, he was gone. I cried for joy all the way back to the cottage.

I have never stopped praising God for sending that angel (I hope to see him face to face some day to thank him). In my excitement I didn't even think to pray and ask for God's help. But that angel was watching over us and responded. God is so good, and we are so grateful. Many thanks again.

—D. J. S., Howell, Wisconsin

It was a warm spring day in southern California in 1959. I was fourteen years old and was spending a fun afternoon at the beach with my friends. I was a really skinny girl and not a very strong swimmer. I can't remember which beach we were at or why we were there without adults, but, other than us, the beach was deserted.

My friends and I were happily playing in the water, unaware that we were gradually getting out into deeper and deeper water. When someone finally noticed how far out we were, we decided we had better get back to shore. They were all stronger swimmers than I, and I was quickly outdistanced.

As I was struggling to catch up, I became caught in a riptide. I found myself literally fighting for my life. In all my struggles, I couldn't get away from that spinning water, and I was rapidly losing strength. As I would come up for air, I would scream for my friends, but they were too far away to hear.

I was weakening quickly and came to the realization that my situation was hopeless and that I would drown in the next couple of minutes. Being a Christian, I started praying, not for deliverance, which seemed impossible, but for forgiveness of my sins.

As I mentally prepared myself to die, I suddenly felt a strong hand grab me by the back of my T-shirt. That hand literally yanked me out of the water and into a boat. When I came to my senses, I saw that I was in a small rowboat with two young men. They scolded me for being so foolish and rowed me closer to shore. I could see my friends lying on the beach, basking in the sun, oblivious to my plight. When we got to shallower water, the young men told me to get out of the boat. I staggered up to the beach, yelling to my friends. By then they had realized I was missing and were scanning the ocean with great concern. I sputtered out my story about the riptide and the young men in the boat who had saved me. They said they had seen nothing but me. We all scanned the water, and for as far as we could see, there was no boat and no young men anywhere in sight.

During the past thirty-three years, I have run into several more situations in which I'm sure my life and those of my husband and children have been protected by the hands of angels. Most Christians can say the same. But the story of my experience in 1959 was the most graphic and dramatic because I actually saw and felt them. I have never forgotten it, nor have I taken for granted the love of God who cares enough to hear the cries of a foolish girl and to send His angels to protect her.

—Donna S., Ridgecrest, California

It was the 5th of May (*Cinco de Mayo*) when I decided to try surfing at Tijuana Beach. I had seldom surfed before, and I had never surfed on this beach. I had with me a borrowed surfboard and a wet suit that belonged to my son Stephen.

In retrospect, I had committed two very important and foolish errors. First, I went surfing alone. Second, I didn't tie my surfboard cord to my ankle. Because of these two neglects, I almost had an early demise.

I'm a fairly good swimmer, and I was surfing in the middle of the beach. For some reason, I was drifting very quickly, farther and farther down to the south end of the beach, with the waves

135

becoming very irregular. All of a sudden, I lost hold of my surfboard, and try as I might, I couldn't reach it. The waves were becoming more treacherous as I continued to bob up and down. Without my board, I couldn't go anywhere; the waves were getting to be more than I could handle. I was barely able to bob up for a breath of air before the waves would pull me under again. I was being sucked under and beaten by the waves.

I was so exhausted that I began to see stars twinkling, even though it was daylight. I could go nowhere without taking in large gulps of seawater. There was no one around to hear my screams; I was about a quarter mile away from shore.

I said to the Lord, "What am I going to do now!" My whole life was flashing before me. I was just about to take my last breath when it seemed someone pushed the board toward me. Somehow I was able to pull myself on top of it. This "person" pushed me to the shore, since there was no way I could have had enough energy to get there myself. I managed to crawl out of the water onto dry land. I passed out right there on the beach for about half an hour. After I regained consciousness, I looked around, but no one was in sight. When I got to the street, a man told me that just last week someone had drowned there. It was sobering to think that I could have been another victim.

What really hit home was when I heard the "Voice of Prophecy's" broadcast on angels in August of 1993. When I heard your stories, tears came to my eyes as I realized how my own angel had helped me. I am more determined than ever to serve the Lord in whatever capacity He has for me.

—Thomas S., San Diego, California

I would like to share an experience I had as a nineteen-year-old sailor serving with the United States Navy in the South Pacific during World War II. This happened early in the morning, aboard ship, in November 1943.

I was down in the engine room with the electrician and motor machinist mate. A man appeared to me and told me that I did not belong down there and that I should leave and go up to the topside. Within a very few seconds after I got out on deck, the ship began to sink, and I abandoned ship and jumped into the water. As the ship was sinking and I was swimming away from it, other sailors who also jumped off the ship and were swimming away were sucked down with the ship when it went down. I noticed a piece of board or something floating, and I clung to that until I was rescued several hours later. I was one of only two survivors from a ship that carried approximately one hundred.

I remembered all the other men who were in the engine room with me, and I made an accurate report at a later date about the men who went down with the ship. I did not say anything about the man who spoke to me, because I did not remember who he was, where he came from, or what happened to him after he gave me the warning.

Thinking about this and learning more about the ministry of angels, I believe this was an angel sent by God from heaven to warn me of the terrible danger that I was in. I was about to lose my life as a young teenager. He seemed to appear and after the message to disappear. I praise God for His love and His concern for me that He sent an angel from heaven to save my life.

—Walter E., Richfield, Minnesota

The following story is a classic. It has found its way into several anthologies of angel stories, but often most of the facts are left out.

We thought you'd like to hear the original story, just as it happened to Mrs. Louise Dubay, now deceased, in the early fifties. Here, in her own words, is her amazing story as it was published in *The Review and Herald*, December 22, 1955.

I was living in a little rented cabin in Anchorage, Alaska, with my only son, when we first heard a "Voice of Prophecy" broadcast. We were both Roman Catholics, but we decided to enroll in the Voice of Prophecy Bible course.

Soon the first Voice of Prophecy lessons came by mail, and oh, how we did love those lessons! We could hardly wait for the next lesson to arrive so that we could study and learn more from the Holy Scriptures. Those Bible truths were so wonderful! They stirred our hearts to the very depths and made us resolve to follow Jesus closer than we had ever done before. My son gave up his liquor, and we each promised God that by His help we would lead a Christian life.

About this time, the Voice of Prophecy notified Pastor M. L. Miles of our interest, and he called to help us with our Bible lessons. We loved Pastor Miles from the very first time we met him. He helped us understand many passages in the Holy Scriptures that had been puzzling to us, and it was so easy to accept that which God had written through His holy prophets and apostles.

About this time, my son fell ill with pneumonia, and nothing the doctors were able to do for him was of any avail. In desperation I promised God that if He would only spare my son's life, I would do anything for Him that He wanted me to do. But God's answer was in the negative. It was not best that He stay the hand of the enemy, and my son fell asleep, cradled in my arms. . . .

After his death, I was bitter against God because He had permitted my precious boy to die, but Pastor Miles came to visit me often, and he explained all the passages in the Scriptures about death. Finally, my heart again melted, and I made a new surrender to God.

Now all this time the Catholic priest was coming to see me. He told me that this grief had fallen upon me because I had strayed from the mother church and that if I would only return, all would be forgiven me. In spite of this, I made up my mind that I would trust in God's Word. Then a terrible thing happened to me.

I suffered a stroke and was sent to the only hospital in Anchorage, the Catholic hospital. There I learned that I was suffering from diabetes, and for a time I felt certain I would die. It was several weeks before I was allowed to return to my little cabin. Kind friends from my new church wanted me to live with them, but the thought of dying in any place other than where my son had fallen asleep was a nightmare to me. I insisted on returning to my little home, for I felt certain that I would not live much longer.

Time passed, and to my consternation, I suffered several strokes, each time being hospitalized. The priest pleaded with me, saying, "Louise, all of this trouble has come upon you because you have left the true church, and God wants you to return." But I knew this trouble was being inflicted upon me by the devil, and if I would be true to God, He could and would use me, sick and crippled as I was, to His honor and glory and to the winning of souls for His kingdom. Therefore, I refused to give up my newfound faith in Jesus and His written Word. But the pleas of this priest tore my heart. When one is sick and suffering pain, it is difficult to understand.

Finally, I was again in my little cabin home. It was on a cold morning in February. I was alone and so badly crippled that I could not walk unless I applied hot and cold fomentations to my leg. My cabin was heated by a wood-burning cookstove, and this morning, no one had remembered to visit me and bring in a fresh supply of wood. I could not call for help, because I did not have a telephone. Later, the church members, who have been so kind to me, paid to have a telephone installed. In desperation I began to pray out loud, asking God to help me and send someone to bring my wood in so I could take care of my crippled leg. Never before had I prayed so hard. But no one came.

Finally, the last of the wood was consumed, and the fire in my stove went out. Outside was thirty degrees below zero. The cabin began to chill rapidly, and I realized that unless someone

139

brought me some wood soon, I would freeze to death. So again I prayed earnestly to the Lord, but no one came.

I realized then that in a little while I would freeze, even though I was protected by the bedcovers. But this time I prayed a different prayer. I told the Lord that if it was His will that I freeze to death, it was all right. I was willing.

About this time, the door opened, and in walked a tall young man carrying an armload of wood. He was not dressed like most people dress in Alaska during the winter months. He had on a black hat and a black overcoat. He placed the wood in the woodbin and proceeded to start making a fire in the stove. When he had the fire going good, he put water in my big teakettle and placed the kettle over the fire.

All of this time he seemed to keep his face turned so that I could not see his full face. After putting the kettle over the fire, he turned, went out the door, then shortly afterward returned with another armload of firewood, which he placed in the woodbin with the wood he had brought in before.

I was so frightened, or perhaps I should say, so awed, that I could not say a word. I just sat there and looked at him, wanting to ask him whether he was an angel, but I was afraid to speak. Finally, I asked him that question in my mind, without speaking a word aloud, and when I did this, he turned toward me, smiled, and nodded his head. His face was so noble that I knew he was not from this world. Then he turned again, opened the door, and left me without saying a word.

For a time I sat there like one turned to stone. Finally I thought: *If he is an angel sent from God, there will not be any footprints in the snow outside the door*, and so I forced myself to hobble to the door, opened it, and looked out on the unruffled snow in my yard. There were no footprints in the snow.

Then I forced myself to lean against the side of the doorcasing and looked around to my right, to see whether the snow had been disturbed where my wood was piled directly underneath my front window. No, the snow had not been disturbed in the slightest over or around my little pile of wood. The snow was perfectly smooth and rounded over, just as it always is after a snowstorm.

As I closed the door to my little cabin, I knew that God did love me and that in my extremity He had sent one of His holy angels to my assistance.

Well, Mrs. Dubay goes on to say that after this, the church members installed an oil-burning cookstove in her cabin so she would never be without fuel again.

Isn't it interesting how God has used Mrs. Dubay, in spite of her sickness and disability, to witness for Him all around the world?

Sometimes just a nudge is all that's needed. Josephine Cunnington Edwards was always in demand as a storyteller and had been speaking to the schoolchildren at Quill Lake, Saskatchewan. But a heavy snow had closed down the school. So she went to stay with some friends, the Tataryns, in the town of Canora. The Tataryns lived in the country by a little lake, which was frozen.

We enjoyed the Friday-evening sunset as we ate supper together. Then Mrs. Tataryn showed me to a pretty room with a beautiful, soft bed. I hung up two dresses and went to sleep as sweetly as if I had been in my own bed at home.

Suddenly, at 1:30 a.m., someone tapped me on the shoulder. I got up and looked around, but no one was in the room. I went to the door and opened it, and a surge of gas and poisoned air rushed into my room. I nearly fell over.

In my bare feet and pajamas, I ran down that strange hall screaming, "Something terrible is happening! The air is terrible! Wake up and see!"

Dr. Tataryn opened the door and stood still a minute. "Mrs.

Edwards, get dressed! The house is burning down! No—you won't have time to dress. Get as many of your things as you can!"

His wife got up and woke the two children. Jennifer, their daughter, picked up her frightened cat.

"Go out quickly. We don't have time for anything!"

I had managed to grab a few of my things—my half-filled suitcase, my bag of books, and my shoes. We ran out barefoot into the deep snow and below-zero temperature. Just ten minutes earlier, my guardian angel had awakened me. We saw the lovely house burn up, and if it had not been for our heavenly Father's protective care, we would have been in the midst of the terrible flames.

The next day we thanked our wonderful Lord for His protection. Loving friends invited us to stay with them, and we had our Week of Prayer in Canora.[1]

Sometimes God intervenes even when the situation is not life-threatening. Sometimes He provides emergency help around the home just when it is needed. The first story comes from Darlene F., of Groton, South Dakota. She wrote to us about her friend, Marci.

Marci had recently become a widow. One summer day she decided to fix a leak between her entry roof and her mobile home. She didn't have a long-enough ladder, so she pushed a picnic table against the side of the entry and then placed a short stepladder on top of the picnic table.

Marci, with brush and tar sealer in hand, proceeded up the ladder and onto the roof. When she finished fixing the cracks, she turned around to get off the roof. As she turned to step down the ladder, it fell to the ground.

Looking down the street, Marci didn't see anything. It was mid-afternoon, and her neighbors were all at work. Closing her eyes, she asked God to help her in this situation. Upon opening her eyes, she spotted a tall blond man standing behind her car in her driveway. She yelled out to the man to please come and help her. She shared with him her predicament, ending with, "Would you please pick up the ladder and help me down?"

The man did as he was asked. Marci continued to talk and finally thanked him for his help. She no more than got inside her home when she realized that through it all, the man had not uttered a sound. He had not said a word. She went outside and looked up and down the street but saw no car and no man. The street was as empty as before. She felt as though her rescuer was an angel in disguise and that her prayers had been answered immediately.

There are many stories of car trouble in this book, but here's a story of a woman who needed help before her trip ever got underway. It happened in 1978. Lori K. of Chino Hills, California, had just gotten a new car.

With her husband off to work, Lori was looking forward to a full day of running errands. When she went to open the garage door, it wouldn't open. No amount of pulling would budge it. She went back through the house into the garage and discovered that the spring on the garage door was broken—which explained the bang she had heard a few moments earlier. She was disappointed. How could she run errands with a car trapped in the garage?

Lori went back out the front door and stood there praying, "Lord, show me what to do." Just then, a man walked up. He was a fairly thin, ordinary-looking man, carrying a briefcase.

"Let me get that for you," he said.

"Oh, but the spring is broken."

"Here, I'll hold it up while you back out."

IN THE PRESENCE OF ANGELS

Lori was a little puzzled as he lifted the door, and she ran to the car. Having never driven it before, she jerked her way down the driveway, knocking her papers off the seat and onto the floor. She bent down to pick them up quickly. When she sat up to say "thank you" to her unexpected helper, the garage door was closed, and not a soul was in sight anywhere, up or down the block. Lori writes,

> I guess it didn't hit me at that time what had happened. But when my husband came home, and I told him the story, he tried to open the garage door himself with both hands, and it wouldn't budge at all. My unexpected helper had done it with complete ease and never even set his briefcase down. Nobody can tell me otherwise; this helper was an angel.

Some people question stories like this. After all, why would God work a miracle to open a garage door while allowing millions to perish through injustice and hunger?

But would we want God to intervene only in big things? If so, then He would certainly never have time for our puny individual needs.

Even in Scripture, God sometimes intervenes in trivial matters yet is silent at critical moments. He worked a miracle to enable Elisha's student to recover his borrowed axhead yet failed to save the head of John the Baptist. He preserved the shoes of the Israelites for forty years in the desert and provided wine for the wedding at Cana yet allowed Isaiah and James and Stephen and most of the apostles to die as martyrs.

We serve a God who cares about the little things of our lives. Sometimes He says No to our requests. Sometimes He allows His children to suffer tragedy; while at other times, when we call upon His name, He even saves us from inconveniences. At all times, He knows what is best. He who is the maker of worlds, the God of the galaxies, is also the God of the garage door. Let us praise His name.

---

1. Josephine Cunnington Edwards, "Awakened by an Angel," *Adventist Review,* 17 January 1991, 16.

CHAPTER

10

Lifted by Loving Hands

Though I walk in the midst of trouble, you preserve my life; you stretch out your hand against the anger of my foes, with your right hand you save me (Psalm 138:7).

Save us and help us with your right hand, that those you love may be delivered (Psalm 108:6).

In response to a call on the "Voice of Prophecy" broadcast for modern, true-life angel stories, Guy M. of Warren, Ohio, wrote us the following:

145

IN THE PRESENCE OF ANGELS

I heard you on my radio talking about angels, and I started to cry, since I, too, have been blessed with an angel encounter. My friends and I were climbing a high hill one day in October of 1974. I was in front when the ground gave way where I was standing. A huge person grabbed me in midair, and I was in the air for about thirty seconds. I felt like I was falling in slow motion, and when I hit the ground, it felt soft like a pillow, not hard. My friends couldn't believe it; they said I was floating through the air.

Hard to believe? There is a promise in the Bible that just fits that story and others in this chapter. It's found in Psalm 91:11, 12:

> He will command his angels concerning you to guard you in all your ways; they will lift you up in their hands, so that you will not strike your foot against a stone.

Here are some other reports from people who never actually saw an angel—they only *felt* one as they were lifted out of the way of danger by loving angel hands.

Roscoe Swan of Roseburg, Oregon, shared with us a story he heard as a child from a man by the name of Wolcott. One day young Wolcott was helping the men put up hay. They had loaded the hay wagon high, and he was to take it to the barn while the men continued their work in the field. He took hold of the reins as he sat high on the hay near the front of the load, guiding the horses as they pulled the wagon down the hill toward the barn.

As the wagon neared the gate, Wolcott was somehow thrown forward and found himself falling between the wagon and the horses. He saw the hooves swinging out behind the horses and realized that he was about to come down onto those steel-shod "kicking" hooves! To make matters worse, he saw that he would land in front of the right wagon wheel, and he could visualize that wheel rolling over him and crushing him. Then something grabbed him, lifted him up, and set him back on the top of the hay, back where he had been before falling off! And he rode there safely to the barn, thanking the Lord for His protection.

Roscoe was an adolescent when he heard this story from Mr. Wolcott. We publish very few third-person accounts, but this story is by way of introduction to one that happened to Roscoe himself several years later while working at a furniture shop.

One Friday afternoon he was helping to unload a truckload of plywood, stacking the bundles against the wall. Eventually, the stack became so high that Roscoe had to toss the bundles to get them onto the top of the stack. As he turned his back to get another bundle, a strange feeling came over him. Looking back over his shoulder, with a thrill of horror, he saw the whole wall of plywood coming his way!

The next thing he knew, there was a huge, disorderly pile of plywood several feet deep spreading over a good portion of the floor, and he was standing on top of the pile, completely unhurt! Apparently his guardian angel had picked him up and held him safely above the falling bundles so that not a single one had touched him and had then set him down safely on top of the pile!

His wife had a similar experience when she was a girl. She and a neighbor girl were sitting cross-legged on the dirt road that went by her father's farm in Minnesota. They weren't worried about traffic, because they were many miles from any highway, and cars rarely came by. Those that did usually traveled rather slowly.

But suddenly a car came around a nearby curve at high speed, heading right for the girls. They did not have time to move out of the way. But the next thing they knew, they were sitting cross-legged on the grass by the side of the road. They were sitting in the same position they had been in only a moment before when they were on the road.

Later experimentation proved that moving quickly from that position was impossible. Evidently their guardian angels must have moved them to preserve their lives.

Naomi H. and her husband, Charlie, tell essentially the same story, second verse. They were shopping for a few things for their new apartment in downtown Orlando, Florida. They had crossed one street and were waiting at the light to cross the intersection to their left. They were standing below the curb, when suddenly they were whisked from that gutter up onto the curb, and immediately a big city bus brushed by, not more than six inches from their noses.

Naomi looked at Charlie and said, "Did you see that bus coming?"

He said, "No, didn't you pull me up on the curb?"

She said, "No, didn't you pull me up?"

"No."

They looked around them and found that they were the only visible persons on that corner.

Same story, third verse. This time it happened to John L. of Ontario, California:

> One day in 1946, I was downtown in Los Angeles, where I had dined for lunch at Cliftons, on South Olive Street.
>
> I was at the corner of Olive and 7th Street, and I was preparing to cross the street. As the light turned green, all at once I was lifted up in the air, and I landed on my feet back on the sidewalk; everyone thought I had been hit by a large Mack truck. This all took place in a mere second.
>
> When I turned around to look behind me, there was a large silver hand on my shoulder, about five times the size of an ordinary human hand.

The Mack truck was passing by when I landed back on the sidewalk. Had the truck hit me, I would have been killed instantly.

It would seem that God's children should be more careful when crossing the road. This invisible-hand-pulled-me-out-of-traffic episode seems to be a bit too common. Please do not step into the path of an oncoming truck to test this theory. Angels have enough to do already.

Dorrie L. of Yakima, Washington, watched it happen to her daughter. This story took place in Mabton, Washington, in the fall of 1971.

Terri, who was almost four, lived with her parents and younger sister on a country road that was used as a truck route. There were times when the road was very busy with big eighteen-wheelers whizzing by. Other times, the road was very quiet, with no sign of traffic, as it was at the time our story took place.

Looking up at mother with big, pleading eyes, Terri asked for the fifth time, "Mommy, can I please go get the mail all by myself today?" And for the fifth time, Mother said, "Wait until you're a little older."

Drawing herself up to her full height and looking as angelic as she could, Terri said, "But, Mama, you said I'm a big girl, and I'm a real help to you."

Taking a look at the highway and seeing no traffic, Mother gave in because for one so young, Terri was a very responsible child.

Taking Terri by the hand, Mother walked to the front porch. "I'll wait here for you. Go now, while there's no traffic."

Terri walked to the edge of the lawn, stopped, looked both ways, and seeing the road was clear, she walked across the road, reached up, opened the mailbox, took out the mail, closed the box, turned around, and looked in both directions. Seemingly out of nowhere, a big eighteen-wheeler was coming very fast down the road. Now, Terri could have run and made it safely across the road, but she wanted Mother to know she would obey the rules of crossing the road, so she stood by the mailbox and waited. The big truck was so close as it passed Terri, and it made such a strong wind, that it terrified her.

Forgetting about the rules of crossing the road, Terri now began to cry. She saw Mother standing on the porch waiting for her and decided that was where she wanted to be. With one goal in mind, she started across the highway. What Terri didn't know, but Mother could plainly see, was a pickup truck following close behind the first truck, with her precious daughter directly in its path. There was no time to pray, only to comprehend what was happening.

With a cry, Mother covered her eyes, not wanting to watch, but for some unknown reason, she felt the need to see what was happening. Dropping her hands limply at her side, she stood watching, waiting for the pickup to run over her daughter.

There was Terri, running with all her might, arms outstretched, calling, "Mommy, Mommy," and wanting only to get to Mother. The pickup truck, traveling at least fifty miles an hour, was not more than five or six feet from her daughter. There was a look of horror on the driver's face. Then, while Terri's arms were outstretched to her mother and her feet were going forward, it seemed that she was pulled backward, and she was again standing beside the mailbox. The driver, realizing that he had barely missed the child, stepped on the gas, fleeing the scene.

Terri didn't realize what a close call she had had until Mother explained it to her. Then both mother and daughter knelt in a prayer of praise to their Father in heaven.

Perhaps it is not stretching God's promise too far to claim that when we are in the midst of traffic, "even there your hand will guide me, your right hand will hold me fast" (Psalm 139:10).

Here's a different version of "Why did the Christian cross the road?" This story comes from Bonnie H. of Rush, Kentucky.

My husband and I, along with my two daughters, Jane and Emilie, operate two successful antique shops and a restaurant. On August 19, 1992, my daughters and I were on a plane in Cincinnati waiting for takeoff. We were feeling happy that evening since it was our semi-annual buying trip to our favorite city, "The Big Apple."

On this particular evening, Emilie said, "Mama, let's pray." So the three of us joined hands and began to thank God and praise His name. We asked that He send His angels to keep us out of danger on our trip.

On the last day of our trip, things were very hectic, and we were running out of time. While Jane went to a showroom to place an order, Emilie and I dashed to another area to do some last-minute buying.

As we were standing at a very busy intersection, I heard a voice (which I thought was Emilie's) say, "Let's go," in a very impatient tone. As I quickly stepped into the moving traffic, I felt an arm grab me from behind with such swiftness that I couldn't help but fall back against this man's arm. A passing cab missed me by not more than an inch.

I looked up, and his waist was almost level with my eyes. He was wearing navy slacks and a navy shirt. Looking up at his head, I thought, how neat his hair was—so perfectly trimmed.

My next awareness was Emilie's voice saying, "Thanks for saving her life," and I joined in by saying, "Yes, thank you." Looking for him as I spoke, I realized that he had disappeared. Ellie J. has a traffic story too, but she wasn't pulled back; she was pushed forward. She was trying to cross a very busy four-lane street in downtown Salem, North Carolina, when she felt the hands of God or His angel. She was only one-third of the way across the street when the light changed. She was in a wheelchair, so she called on Jesus to help. Immediately, she felt someone come up behind her and take the handles of her wheelchair and push her quickly to the other side and up a store driveway. She turned around in her wheelchair to thank her benefactor, but there was no one to be seen anywhere behind her.

Geraldine C. of Lexington, Kentucky, wasn't crossing the road; she was driving on it, behind a lumber truck on her way to church. The truck was carrying thick, heavy sheets of lumber. She was driving the speed limit (55), but the truck was moving a bit faster. She writes:

> All of a sudden, a sheet of lumber came off the truck and was heading straight toward my windshield. My first thought was, *It's going to cut off my head!* I could do nothing but cry, "Jesus, Jesus, Jesus!"
>
> Just as the sheet of lumber reached my windshield, two hands went under it, lifting it over the top of my car. It came down on the back, doing only minor damage. I went to church in shock. When I shared what had happened, everyone was excited and agreed that God surely sent angel hands to protect me. I give Him thanks and praise.

Let's get out of traffic for a while and look at some more stories of people who have felt the hand of God in other dangerous places. The following story comes from Harriet F., of Brinkley, Arkansas.

One particular Sunday morning a couple of months ago, I felt full of happiness and joy as I dressed for church. I started from the bathroom to my bedroom only to find the doorway blocked by one of my cats. In my excitement, I tried to jump over the cat. My foot caught on the door, and the immediate pain doubled me over. I grabbed the door for support and began to pray that I would make it to the bed without passing out. I straightened up slightly and saw a man's arm reaching out to me for support. I took hold of the arm and began walking, still hunched over, to the bed.

My thirteen-year-old daughter, Cathy, was in my bedroom and said, "Mom, do you need some help? Are you OK? I didn't answer her because of the intense pain, but I thought the question was puzzling since I already had someone helping me. I sat on the bed and began to look at my foot, which was swelling and turning purple. When I finally looked up, nobody was standing there except Cathy. I heard my husband Don clanking the dishes in the kitchen, and I thought he had just gone in there.

It wasn't until later in the day that I told Don, "I sure am glad you were there when I hit my foot to help me to the bed."

He said, "Honey, I wasn't there; I was in the kitchen washing dishes." I then assumed it was my nineteen-year-old son Mike.

I told him, "Mike, I sure am glad you were there to help me to the bed when I hit my foot."

He said, "Mom, I wasn't there; I was outside cleaning out the car."

It was then that I realized I had been visited by an angel. Cathy said that she saw nobody but that I was walking strangely, as if I were holding onto someone's arm. I have no doubts, and I praise the Lord for the angel who helped me.

A shopping mall is the setting for this next story from Margaret P., of Calgary, Alberta. She gave her life to Jesus at age twelve in England. After walking with Him for seventy-five years, she was lifted with angel hands.

On November 6, 1990, at 7:30 p.m., Margaret was in Market Mall Shopping Center by herself. She was approaching the up escalator, and just about to step on, when a young mother stepped in front of her. She had a baby in her arms, along with many parcels. She moved onto the escalator and left her tiny daughter standing behind, afraid to step on.

The mother went on up, so Margaret said to the daughter, "Come, take my hand, and we'll go up together." After they were on the escalator, hand in hand, the girl pulled forward to get to her mother, and Margaret lost her balance and fell flat with one arm under her. Meanwhile, the mother and child went on up and left her behind. She lay there and kept repeating, "I can't get up." She began to wonder what she would do at the top of the escalator, which, except for herself, was empty.

Suddenly, two hands came through her heavy coat and under her arms and lifted her and stood her perfectly upright and poised. She felt a being pass by her and go in front of her and disappear in a soft mist. She started to go after him to say "thank you," when a voice said very quietly, "Don't look for him."

So she turned and walked quietly away and started singing to herself the hymns "Love Lifted Me" and "He Touched Me."

Margaret writes, "I never heard his voice, nor did I see his face, but the Lord let me see in my spirit. Those hands! They were beautiful hands—so perfect and so clean. The whole experience took only a few minutes. But it has been a beautiful experience to me."

When General Larry Fuller, Assistant Deputy Judge Advocate of the U.S. Army, checked into Walter Reed Hospital, he was diagnosed with cancer, requiring an operation that would leave him with a colostomy. But a later examination found no trace of cancer. What happened in between is a fascinating story.

General Fuller did not believe in God. As an atheist, he felt no need for divine intervention. But God intervened anyway.

On the night before his surgery, which was scheduled only two days after the diagnosis, the general was lying on his back in bed at home, wide awake. Suddenly, the ceiling opened up, and a huge, visible hand reached down from the sky and into his abdominal cavity. The general felt a change and knew that he was healed. The next day, tests revealed no traces of the cancer.

General Fuller could not understand what had happened to him, so he began to study. His study led him to become a baptized believer in Jesus Christ.

This raises a question. Why would God heal an atheist unsolicited while leaving hundreds of praying, believing Christians to die of cancer?

In fact, angelic visitations seem to bear little relationship to saintliness. Could it be that God has less reason to protect His own from temporal tragedy than He does to protect those who are not yet His? After all, His children have an eternal life of joy to look forward to. The death of a Christian is, in the light of eternity, not as tragic as the death of an unbeliever, for whom death is eternal.

Therefore, given a choice between healing an unbeliever and healing a believer, it is to God's advantage to heal the unbeliever, for this widens the window of opportunity for that person to be in heaven. And God wants to get as many of His children into heaven as He can.

Then there is the fascinating story of Franz Hasel. He never saw an angel, but, like Roscoe Swan, he was lifted up by one. Actually, there is much more to this thrilling story than we have space for here. We call it "The Nazi Who Wouldn't Fight."

Franz was an active Seventh-day Adventist pastor in Germany at the beginning of World War II. He was a man who cherished peace, and when he received his draft notice, he was deeply disturbed.

IN THE PRESENCE OF ANGELS

Franz gathered his family around him and prayed. "Lord, keep me faithful to Your Word and to the truth." Then he prayed for his family, and he repeated the promise of Matthew 28, "Lo, I am with you always, even unto the end of the world."

When Franz reported to his commanding officer, he requested to be assigned to the medical corps. The officer, correctly suspecting that he did not wish to carry a weapon, asked him a trick question. "Let us imagine you are in combat. One of your fellow soldiers is wounded, and the enemy is advancing on you and your comrade. Would you use your weapon to defend your wounded comrade?"

Franz said, "I would lay my body on my wounded comrade to protect him." It was clear to the officer that Franz would not use the weapon.

The commanding officer said to him, "We do not need cowards in the medical corps."

Franz was issued a pistol and sent to the front. Eventually, he threw away his pistol, and in its place he wore a piece of wood carved and painted to look like a revolver. As a follower of Jesus, Franz was convinced that his business was to save life, not to kill. And God miraculously opened the way for him to serve without killing anyone all during his five-and-a-half years in the army.

Franz was sent to Poland. He was assigned to a battalion whose task was to build bridges for the German tanks to cross the rivers. They were always at the front. There were two thousand men in that battalion, and they were replaced three times. So fierce was the fighting that, of the original group, only Franz and six others survived.

After Franz got out of the frying pan of Poland, he was plunged into the fire of Russia. His unit was among the invading forces on the southern flank of the German advance. While the center marched on Moscow, a smaller force was sent into the Caucasus, where they were to capture the oil fields. Franz's unit was assigned to capture the city of Baku on the Caspian Sea.

The military unit in which Franz was serving was not able to continue toward their objective. Tank unit after tank unit was withdrawn to help the troops trying to take Stalingrad. Only a few units with a few tanks and pieces of artillery were left in the little village in the Caucasus Mountains, where Franz was.

Slowly the Russian winter took its toll, and the war began to turn against Germany. While the Germans were losing the battle of Stalingrad, Franz's unit was three hundred miles deeper into Russia, southeast of Stalingrad. He was beginning to wonder if he would ever get out. Would he ever see his family again?

One night he prayed, "Lord, please give me a special sign to let me know whether I'll ever see my children and my wife again." And then he fell asleep.

Franz was an early riser. Early the next morning, about 4:00 or 4:30, he heard a frighteningly familiar sound. It was the distant rumble and squeak of approaching tanks. All around him on the floor lay sleeping soldiers. Across the street from the schoolhouse, the Russians had built a lookout tower. Franz climbed up as quickly as he could and looked in the direction from which the sounds were coming. What he saw made his blood run cold. Dozens and dozens of Russian T-34 tanks were grinding slowly but relentlessly toward the village. He clambered quickly down and raced across the field, shouting, "Get up! Get up quick! The Russians are coming!"

There was a mad scramble for the door. Suddenly, Franz remembered that he was in charge of the secret documents, but there was no time to get them together and take them along. There was a door to a side room in the schoolhouse with a key in it. Quickly bundling the documents together, he tossed them in, locked the door, and drew a skull and crossbones on the door with a piece of chalk, along with the words *DANGER! DO NOT ENTER.* He stuffed the key in his pocket and ran out the door, only to find that his comrades were already gone. He was left behind.

Looking around in desperation, he spied the last German tank just beginning to move, about 150 yards away. It was pulling a heavy piece of artillery. *If I don't make a dash for it*, thought Franz, *I'll be left behind. I'll be a prisoner of war to the Russians. That will be the end of me.*

IN THE PRESENCE OF ANGELS

So Franz ran for his life. He didn't quite reach the tank, but he just managed to jump onto the connecting tow bar between the tank and the cannon. At that moment, that tank was going around a sharp bend. It jerked backward, and Franz felt himself falling. There was nothing to grab to hold on. As he hit the road, he saw the cannon wheel coming toward his head. He had fallen in such a position that he couldn't roll to one side or the other.

Franz later told the story this way: "I saw my whole life, from my earliest moment until that time, like a big movie screen in my mind. I prayed. All I had time to say was, 'Lord! Save me and my family!'" Just as he expected to be crushed by the cannon wheel, someone grabbed him in the back, jerked him out, lifted him up in the air, and plopped him right smack on the turret hatch of that German tank.

Who picked me up? he wondered. He looked around, but no one was there. Then he remembered his prayer of the night before. Of course! God had answered his prayer. "Thank You, Lord," he whispered, "for saving my life. And, Lord, thank You, because now I know I'll see my family again."

Franz firmly believed that an angel of the Lord saved him because the Lord still had a work for him to do.

Franz had a commanding officer who was slowly losing his eyesight. There were no glasses to be had there at the Russian front. One day the officer said, "Tell me, Franz, what can I do? I see so badly. When I try to look through the binoculars, I can barely see."

"That's simple," said Franz. "Eat carrots."

"Now are you insulting me?" replied the officer. "I do not usually eat rabbit food! Eat carrots? Are you serious?" But Franz assured him he was serious and explained the rationale for his advice. Sure enough, the man followed his counsel, and his eyesight improved. From that moment on, there was an emotional bond between Franz and this commanding officer.

One day this officer asked a bigger question. "What future, Franz, do you think we'll have?"

That was a loaded question. In the German army, one just didn't say, "We are losing the war." It might have cost him his life. The German high command kept promising that new weapons would soon turn the course of the war in their favor.

So Franz answered very cautiously. "I want to ask you a question. Are you asking me privately, or are you asking me officially?"

"I'm asking you privately."

"Well," said Franz, "I have a Book here." And he took out his little Bible and turned to Daniel 2, and he said, "I want to tell you something. The German Reich is never going to conquer the world. That's what this little Book tells me."

Franz proceeded to tell him how the prophecy predicts the empire of the ancient Babylonians, followed by the Medo-Persians, then Greece, and then Rome, and how the prophecy indicates that we are now living down in the toes of clay. It clearly spells out that no earthly kingdom will ever again rule the world. The next great kingdom will be the kingdom of Jesus Christ.

Now it happened that in that army unit, there was an officer who had been a professor of history from the University of Frankfurt. "I want to check on your history," his friend said. Franz had to repeat everything in the presence of this other officer. And at every date the first officer would ask his historian friend, "Is this the correct date?"

"Yes."

"Did such and such a battle occur?"

"Yes."

"Was Cyrus the first king of Medo-Persia?"

"Yes." It all checked out. Only Franz did not tell this other officer the bottom line—that Germany could never win.

From that moment on, the army officer began saving gasoline so that the entire unit would be able to drive all the way back from the Soviet Union to Germany.

In the summer of 1945, the day finally came when Franz's unit drove all the way back into Austria and became prisoners of war of the Americans. German intelligence had discovered that if they wanted to get into American territory, they had to cross a particular river in Austria. They wanted to avoid having to surrender to the Russians at any cost, so they made a run to get across that river and made it just half an hour before it was closed. And so Franz Hasel became a prisoner of war of the Americans.

When the German soldiers surrendered, they were detained as prisoners of war until their complicity in the atrocities of war could be sorted out. For many of the prisoners, this took months or years. Some of Franz's relatives were shipped off to the United States and detained there for two or three years. But Franz was a prisoner for only ten days!

In West Germany, Franz Hasel was the first minister to return from the war and to start again. He could praise the Lord for His wonderful care and for His promise: "Lo, I am with you always, even unto the end of the world."

In some areas along the Russian front, only 1 to 2 percent of the German soldiers who entered Russia ever returned to their homes. Franz Hasel was among that small percentage. He came home after being away in the German army for five-and-a-half years. How lucky the Hasel family felt. Many of the children in the area where they lived had fathers or brothers who didn't come home. But no member of the Hasel family was lost in the war.

Franz Hasel's children have grown up with a strong faith and trust in God. "Now I know," they can say, "that the Lord saves his anointed; he answers him from his holy heaven with the saving power of his right hand" (Psalm 20:6).

Scripture says, "Them that honor me I will honor." And God is just as willing and able to save today as ever. "Surely the arm of the Lord is not too short to save, nor his ear too dull to hear" (Isaiah 59:1).

Maybe you've never felt angel hands. The authors haven't. But we believe that for those who love God, throughout all of the ups and downs of life, underneath us are the everlasting arms. And when we get to heaven, we want to see those strong hands that have invisibly guided and protected us all of our lives, don't you?

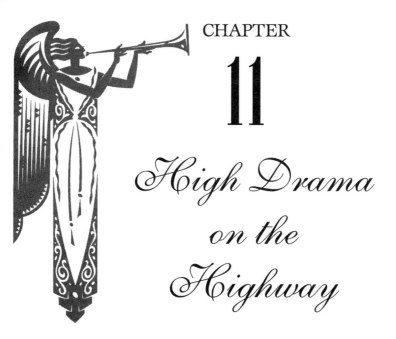

CHAPTER

11

High Drama on the Highway

Maybe he was an angel, maybe not. But after Margaret K., of Knoxville, Tennessee, ran out of gas on an interstate on-ramp, a man drove up in a small gray car. He got out, carrying a cardboard funnel in his hand, saying that since her car used unleaded gas, he would help her.

He was so beautiful, says Margaret, he looked unreal. His skin was golden looking, his hair was dark, and his clothes were immaculate, and he had a beautiful gold watch on. He appeared to be in his thirties (makes you wonder if some angels aren't more fashion conscious

161

than others, doesn't it?).

After he helped her put the gas in her car and turned to leave, he said, "God bless you."

She replied, "God bless you too, sir." When Margaret looked up after the man had gotten into his car, he was gone.

Ever since human beings began to travel, it seems that God has had something like a Seraphic Traveler's Aid Resource (STAR), and today it's busier than ever.

We might mention a few early STAR projects. When Abraham sent his servant on a journey to find a wife for his son, he told him, "The Lord, before whom I have walked, will send his angel with you and make your journey a success" (Genesis 24:40). In Exodus 23:20, God tells Moses, "See, I am sending an angel ahead of you to guard you along the way and to bring you to the place I have prepared."

When Sarah, Abraham's wife, forced him to send her maidservant Hagar away, Hagar ended up stranded alone in the desert with her son Ishmael, facing an uncertain future. The story is told in Genesis 21. When the water ran out and Ishmael was in danger of dehydration, an angel of the Lord appeared and found water for them.

When Elijah fled into the wilderness and collapsed from exhaustion, an angel twice tapped him on the shoulder and awakened him to a cooked meal, saying, "Get up and eat, for the journey is too much for you" (1 Kings 19:7).

Wherever God's children go, God's angels go with them. Since travelers lack many of their normal resources, they need extra help. Sometimes they are stranded or hungry or endangered. Sometimes they get lost—and seeking the lost is a favorite pastime in heaven. God does not change; He is the same yesterday, today, and forever, and He still cares for travelers.

But today there is much more travel, so business is booming at STAR. The invention of the automobile seems to have opened a whole new world of opportunities for these tireless do-gooders (what we call "problems" I believe angels call "opportunities"). When in trouble, just remember this jingle: you can trust your car to the man who comes from STAR.

We received the following story from Norma L., of Corvallis, Oregon, shortly after a "Voice of Prophecy" broadcast on angels:

Listening to your broadcast today, I was reminded of an episode that happened to my daughter and me a few years ago. It was a very dark Sunday night, and we were coming back to Corvallis from Salem, where we had visited my mother-in-law.

The highway was crowded with speeding cars swishing by us. Suddenly, the headlights of our Jeep went out, leaving us in total and dangerous darkness. I turned on the faint right-hand turn signal, looking for some place to stop, but there were only exit lanes and no shoulders. As the turn signal continued to tick, I asked my eleven-year-old daughter to keep her eyes peeled for a suitable stopping place.

Meanwhile, cars continued to speed by, with no signs of a police car in sight. I didn't want to panic, so I prayed for guidance, protection, and serenity in that distressing situation. After about fifteen miles of that blind driving, we spotted a gas station far to the right of the highway. Driving carefully so we would not fall in the ditch, we made it to the lighted building.

Right away, a young man dressed in gas-station white overalls, with a gasoline brand on his uniform, came toward us and asked, "May I help you?"

Relieved, I said, "Certainly! Thank you. The headlights are

out, and we've been driving in the dark!"

He didn't say anything but placed both hands on the hood of the Jeep, and immediately, the lights came to life, bright and glowing. He did nothing else!

"Oh, thank you, thank you!" we said. "How much do we owe you?"

"Nothing," he said. Again, we thanked him and went around the station to get back on the highway. The headlights were brightly shining!

As we rounded the building, we saw an older man sitting in the office, reading a newspaper, so we stopped. I said, "Sir, we were in a predicament, and your nice assistant was so kind to help us that I wanted to thank you too."

He replied, "Sorry, but I don't have any assistants. I work here alone!"

My daughter and I couldn't believe it! We protested, "But we saw him; he helped us!"

"No, ladies, I am alone here!"

Then my daughter and I knew that our guardian angel had come to our rescue. There can be no other explanation. Never again did the Jeep's lights fail us.

God's angel mechanics are specialists in starting stalled cars. Often they don't seem to need any tools.

Sometime ago, Mrs. Ruby S., of Avon Park, Florida, and a friend were traveling from Palm Beach to Orlando, Florida. Their car stopped near Sebastian Inlet and would not start. Shortly a young man came along on a motorcycle and, using a piece of wire from his motorcycle bag, fixed the car so it would run. He told the women not to let it stop until they reached their destination, as it would not start again.

They started the car and turned to thank the man, but he and his motorcycle were not to be seen anywhere. There had been no sound of the motorcycle starting either.

When they reached Orlando, the car would not start again. A competent mechanic looked at the car and said no car could run wired up as that one had been!

Christine B., of Fort Wayne, Indiana, was driving a car that stalled at the most inopportune times. One day, it stalled as she was crossing the railroad tracks. She did everything she could to start the engine, but to no avail. The dog in the back seat began to bark furiously, and when she turned, she saw a switch engine backing down toward her. She had no time to get out, so there was nothing to do but pray.

The engine never did start—but the car did! It rolled silently across the tracks with no apparent means of locomotion. Christine believes her guardian angel was there.

As she cleared the tracks, she saw the horrified look on the engineer's face; it had been that close. She coasted to the curb and had to leave the car there. She writes, "The wonder of that miracle has never left me and has influenced my life."

Stalled cars seem to be one of a woman's worst fears. Men have problems with cars too. Take Mr. George S., of Fletcher, North Carolina, for example.

One afternoon, I drove six miles from Englewood, Colorado, to the Denver railroad station. After completing my errand, I returned to my car but was unable to start it. People were leaving from work, but I didn't want to ask strangers for a push.

When no one was outside the station, I walked in. The only person present was the ticket agent. I didn't believe he would leave his post to aid me, so I started toward the door.

A very tall man passed me. I returned to my auto and stood in front of it. The tall man came out of the building, approached me, and asked, "Are you having trouble?" I told him my predicament.

"Do you have a screwdriver?"

"Yes," I said, and I opened the door to get it just as this man brought one from his car.

"Start your engine." As I turned the key, he touched the engine with the screwdriver, and it immediately started. Keeping my foot on the gas pedal, I thanked him and drove off.

After I arrived home, I told my father, whose car I had used, of my experience. Though he was a good mechanic, he couldn't restart the engine.

A finite man doesn't start a car by touching the engine with a screwdriver. I was so sorry I hadn't had enough presence of mind to shake hands with the angel while thanking him, for I am positive my guardian angel performed a miracle in front of my eyes to help me return home!

Then there's the time Dorothy M., of Fillmore, California, needed a quick jump start in the middle of traffic, and God sent His mechanics to help.

After a long, grueling day at the office, a very tired Dorothy headed toward the K Mart on the way home. As she began to climb a small hill, her engine died.

Oh no, she thought, *not this!* But efforts to start the car were fruitless. To make matters worse, several horns behind her were blaring impatiently. Dorothy was seized with panic. Her brain refused to work. With a line of honking cars behind her, she felt like crawling into a hole.

Suddenly a thought came: *Why not try prayer?* She sent up an earnest plea to God for help. Then she quickly stepped out of the car, but before she could even close the door, a young man appeared as if from nowhere. He climbed in while another young man motioned for her to get off the pavement. She walked over to the side of the road.

Almost instantly the car started, and she hurriedly followed it as it was being driven up the grade to a nearby parking space. Just as she caught up, the young man was stepping out of the car.

In awe she looked at these two well-dressed, handsome young

men with blond hair. A holy glow seemed to radiate from their faces. Breathlessly, Dorothy said to them: "My, you both must come from very fine homes." Neither said a word, but they nodded their heads in affirmation as they exchanged smiles.

Dorothy reached down to get her purse, which was lying on the car floor, so she could offer to pay them for their kindness. When she turned to face them, they were nowhere in sight. She climbed into her car and sat there in dumbfounded amazement as the implications of what she had just seen dawned on her. Were these two young men human beings, or were they angels? She still wonders.[1]

Sometimes it seems God *causes* cars to stall, as Isle K., of Santa Rosa, California, discovered.

My brother Hans lived in Africa as a missionary. He was a very good mechanic. He used to say that he was the only missionary who was not in debt. That was because he could fix his own car. The others had to have their cars towed from two hundred to five hundred miles to get them repaired.

One day they were going to start out on a trip, and they wanted to leave very early, before sunrise, to get a good start. The car wouldn't start. Hans got a lantern and looked. He couldn't find anything wrong, but it wouldn't start. He finally said that they would have to wait until the sun came up so he could get a better look.

When the sun came up, he tried the starter one more time, and it started right up. There was nothing wrong with the car. Later, they discovered that the bridge up ahead was washed out. In the dark, before sunrise, they would not have been able to see it. They believe that God spared their lives, perhaps by sending an angel mechanic to keep the car from starting.

IN THE PRESENCE OF ANGELS

In the late 1980s, Mrs. Helen T., of Frazer, Pennsylvania, was strongly impressed to offer to ride along with her neighbor friend, whose car had been giving her trouble. Her friend drove sixty miles to Easton, Pennsylvania, to visit her son every month. On the way home from this particular trip, the car stalled on a turnpike entrance and refused to start. Several men helped them push the car to a nearby lot on the side of the road.

We sat there for a while, got out, raised the hood, looked in the gas tank, and got back in the car with my little girl on the back seat. I was praying silently, "Dear God, we need help. Send an angel. Yes, dear Jesus, send us an angel." And in a very few minutes, a small truck with the word *Mazda* on the back pulled to the side of the road and stopped, and my friend said, "Are we really going to get some help?"

The man got out of the truck and looked toward us, then slowly walked to the other side of his truck as though to open a door. When she called to him and asked him if he knew anything about cars, he came over to us. He was about six feet tall, and I have never seen any man who could compare to him—a strong, well-built man, with blond hair.

She told him when she turned the key the engine wouldn't turn over. He didn't say a word, but as he stood there, she turned the key, and it started right up and kept running. When she thanked him, he just smiled and quietly walked in front of the car and to the right of the parking area. When I waved and smiled to him, he waved back, but he did not say one word, and he didn't go back to the little Mazda truck, which would have been the natural thing to do.

On the way home, when she stopped at a second turnpike entrance, we had no problem. But she said quietly, "We're leaking gas; keep praying." And we arrived home safely.

When she took her car to the garage, they told her what the trouble was—gas leaking on the manifold. The car could have exploded, killing all three of us.

Donald A. of Knoxville, Tennessee, wasn't quite so lucky—or was he? The gas that leaked onto his manifold actually did catch fire. It happened in the middle of a parking lot. Donald raised the hood and attempted to smother the flames with anything at hand, such as rags and insulation, but to no avail.

Several long minutes of frantic action and thoughts of a hundred cars in flames produced the exclamatory prayer "Jesus" yelled at the top of his voice. Any observer might have thought he was cursing. A car pulled up. A young man got out and calmly poured a milk jug of water on his engine. Without waiting for thanks, he got in his car and drove away. End of story.

If it's not fire, it's ice. When cars encounter deep snow, angels are sometimes the only help around. Here are three stories about deliverance in a snowstorm. The first one is from Mazie Cooke, of Westlake Village, California.

After World War II, my husband and I, along with ten others from Arizona and California, were sent to Germany to work with a branch of NATO in the defense of the countries in Europe. That was the coldest winder in London and Europe in one hundred years.

Our English friends, Ray and Irene (also part of this project), and their two-year-old daughter, Debbie, planned to spend Christmas together in London.

Most of England was snowed in. Everything was at a standstill. Even food could not be delivered.

Our friends had family in a town called Weymouth. Their

concern prompted them to ask us to join them on a trip to Weymouth.

It was snowing very hard as we left London. As we drove, the drifts became higher and higher. We were making a fresh path, as we no longer saw a road. The white of the snow and the sky blended into one.

A look at the gas gauge showed it was only one-fourth full. As cold as we were, we had to turn the car heater off.

Suddenly, from nowhere, we saw lights shining. A land rover (a sort of a jeep-truck) drove up behind us. Three young men jumped out, saying, "Don't go any farther, or you will go over a precipice." They surrounded our little car and turned us around so we could go back to safety.

"Now keep going—we will be right behind you," they said. As we began to move, we looked back—they were gone! There were no tracks in the snow, as we were making fresh ones.

We arrived at the hotel around midnight, going all that way on only a quarter tank of petrol, as it was called. The people at the hotel lighted the fireplace and made us sandwiches and hot coffee.

The headlines in the morning paper read, "Family Freezes to Death on Road to Weymouth." A mother and dad, two children, and a grandmother did not survive.

I sure do believe in angels, but why didn't they see this family that was written about in the paper?

Mazie's question deserves a fuller answer, but the short answer is that angels are not equal-opportunity helpers. They are sent to minister to those who are heirs of salvation (see Hebrews 1:14), and that does not include everybody. Perhaps God saw something special in Mazie.

This does not mean, though, that God always delivers His children from misfortune or that those who are allowed to suffer do not belong to Christ, for sharing in Christ's fellowship of suffering is one of the greatest privileges given to humanity.

High Drama on the Highway

The second snow story comes from Hans Kehney, who allowed us to record his story on tape back in 1982.

It was during the end of March in North Dakota. It began to snow, heavy flakes coming down in large circles forming something like a giant whirlpool. It was twenty-five miles to the nearest highway.

Even though we could no longer see the road, we could feel the ruts that had been formed during the day. Never did we expect the storm to gain such a rapid momentum. The wind howled, and within a half-hour the temperature had dropped to ten below zero. The windshield of the car was covered with heavy ice by now. Our only means of survival was to find a place of shelter. A farm, a home, somewhere.

Halting for a moment, I stepped out of the car, trying to find a mailbox along the road. I took one step, but it was no use, for the wind would have tossed me like a Russian thistle. The fury of the elements was undescribable.

Throwing myself back into the car, I faced my family—my wife and my two little children. We were dressed in light attire. Thus far, I had tried to encourage them to be brave, facing the storm. Now I was ready to burst out, "We're lost. No one but God can help."

For the first time, I heard the children scream. Suddenly, unexpectedly, a light flashed up in front of the car. There stood someone having the form of a man. I rushed out, calling to him, "We are lost. Where is the nearest farm?"

All I remember is that he raised his hand, pointing to the left of where he stood. I climbed back into the car and turned in the direction he had pointed. And up and down we kept on crawling through the terror of darkness.

It must have been all of two miles when the motor began to sputter. We came to a stop just in front of a door. We did not know that we had crossed a farmyard, but we almost drove right into a house.

Inviting us into their home, those dear people just could not believe how we had gotten to their place. "There is no road; the snow is too deep. It is impossible," they said.

In sharing our experience that night in a warm place of shelter, we could not help but agree that it must have been an angel who showed us the way. As far as I remember, thirty-four people perished that night in that section of the prairies of North Dakota. It seemed like the very elements of heaven were shaken. But the lesson we learned is that God is still in control of the elements and of His own, for when times seem to be darkest, God is always near those who have learned the simple lesson of trust.

The snow angels Erma M., of Bryan, Ohio, encountered were some of the liveliest, most playful angels we've heard of, if angels they were. The story begins with Erma losing her bearings in a dizzying whirl of snow. It was nearly midnight, and she still had many miles to go to get home. There were no tire tracks or taillights to follow; the highway seemed deserted. To make matters worse, patches of ice lay beneath the snow.

Suddenly, two large trucks whooshed by, causing her car to slide on a patch of ice. The car lurched to a halt, with the right bumper about a foot from a deep ditch filled with murky water.

Erma pulled her jacket hood up over her head and forced herself out into the bitter wind and snow. She could make out the sound of dogs barking at a house she had passed. As she plodded toward the sound, she began to discern the lights from the farmhouse; then she heard someone calling. It was the farmer's daughter, her father close behind. Erma continues:

They agreed it would take more than manpower to get my car onto the road. We returned to the house, and by this time, I learned of my location. *Why, my pastor lives not too far cross-country*, I thought. *He knows how to handle cars. He'd have me out in no time.*

When I placed the call to their home, his wife answered groggily. When I told her of my predicament, she told her husband, who answered, "Tell her we'll start to pray!" Pray! I fumed to myself. I needed their help, not prayer! But God bless him—he believed in miracles, and so pray he did.

After a lengthy discussion, the farmer offered to attempt to drive me on home. I could rescue my car the next day. It sounded like a good solution, so I trudged back to the car to get some things and lock up.

Just as I was leaning over to lock a door, an approaching vehicle slowed down and pulled into the farmer's driveway, blocking him in. As the four doors flew open, a number of young boys jumped out. Nervously, I jumped in the car and locked my door. No telling what was afoot here, plus I was now totally alone.

Like a well-trained army, they descended on my car, laughing and having a great time in the snow. As I started my car, I heard a voice outside say clearly, "Straighten your wheels!" That's all they said, and that's all I did. So quickly, so effortlessly, my car was back on the highway!

Now with my headlights on, I saw how neat and clean they were all dressed. Two fell on the ice and lay rolling in laughter. I couldn't help wondering why they were out on a night like this. As I watched them, I saw them make a U-turn in their car and go back the way they had come. It was as if they had been dispatched here! Yes, dispatched here to rescue me!

As I rolled down my window to call out my thanks, I noted something else—the foreign license plate. Was this all my imagination? Was this really happening to me? Were those boys mortals or not?

Some folks may call it all a coincidence, but as for me, I want to thank the preacher for a prayer well said and heaven for a prompt and amazing answer!

IN THE PRESENCE OF ANGELS

Sometimes all God's children need on the highway (or in life, for that matter) is a little push, or maybe a pull. Here's a group of stories from travelers who have been pushed or towed in very mysterious ways. The first one is a story we recorded on tape in 1982 from Marge Hohensee.

One winter afternoon when I was on my way home from school, I was traveling on the Grand Central Parkway out on Long Island, New York. My squareback Volkswagen all of a sudden lost power, and I just rolled to a dead stop right there on the parkway.

The snow was banked up on both sides of the road higher than my car, and the road was fairly narrow, even though there were two lanes of traffic going in my direction.

I was afraid to get out on the road for fear someone would strike me. But I didn't want to stay in the car, either, for fear of being hit there.

And so I turned to the only Source of help I knew. "Oh, Lord, I'm really needing Your help at this point," I said.

About two minutes later, a blue car pulled up in front of me and backed up, and a tall man in a beautiful gray overcoat got out. He came around to the window and said, "Do you need some help, lady?"

"I sure do," I responded.

So he moved his car to the next exit, which was fifty to one hundred yards up the road, and came back on foot and pushed me in my car to the exit.

When he came to my window, I thanked him profusely, expecting him to get in his car and go on his way, but he began to ask me questions. What was I going to do now? Well, there was a golf course to my right, and I knew that there was a clubhouse on up about a block away, so I told him that I would walk up there and phone someone to come and help me. But that didn't satisfy him. He wondered if there wasn't a garage somewhere in the vicinity, and I said, well, in fact there was on the cross about three miles down the road. "Well, let's go," he said.

So he maneuvered his car in behind me and pushed me those three miles down to the garage.

I swung my car into the parking lot, and as it rolled to a stop, I quickly jumped out to go back and thank this man who had gone way out of his way to help me. But there wasn't anybody there. There was no car, no man; the road was empty.

This happened to me quite some time ago, but I have never forgotten that man's face or that beautiful gray coat he was wearing. And I've wondered many times since if maybe I met my guardian angel.

Terri M., of Wittmann, Arizona, was making a left turn in her Volkswagen Beetle on a busy road, when a cable that goes from the accelerator to the engine broke. Although the car was still running, she couldn't go anywhere. As she quickly said the words, "God, help me," she felt her car being pushed. She looked in the rearview mirror and saw someone in a white truck pushing her, bumper to bumper.

The white truck pushed her to within one block from home. Terri got out of the car to thank the man, but no one was there. Vanished. "After this experience," she writes, "I felt as if the Lord was making me aware of the presence of His angels."

Sometimes angels push; sometimes they pull. Maria J., of Corpus Christi, Texas, and her husband had just left a prayer meeting. They had been there for several hours praising the Lord and left a little after midnight in the midst of a downpour.

Our two children were asleep in the back seat. It was a long trip home and, as usual, we took a back road. All of a sudden, we hit a sinkhole, and our front tire sank all the way in. We both got

175

out in the rain to see the damage. I was four-months pregnant and couldn't help my husband push or move the car.

We got back into the car and prayed. We had only been praying for two minutes when miraculously, a tow truck appeared out of nowhere. And just at the same time, it stopped raining.

This was a back road that rarely had traffic, let alone a tow truck at midnight. The driver, never speaking, just quietly hooked up our car and pulled us out.

As the man unhooked the car, my husband got out to thank him. The man only got back into his tow truck, waved, and left.

As my husband walked back to the car, I got out to join him. We both turned around to look at the tow truck, but it had already disappeared. We were dumbfounded. This back road was five miles long and had no exits anywhere. My husband raced to see if we could catch him to thank him. We drove all five miles and never did find him.

In the *Adventist Review*, March 25, 1986, Hazel A. Jackson tells of how she and her husband were returning from a vacation trip to Death Valley when they lost their brakes.

We had just reached the top of a mountain when my husband said to me, "We have no brakes." My heart seemed to stop!

We were driving a heavy car, pulling a travel trailer, and were already gaining speed down the mountain. On one side of us was the abrupt drop, with huge boulders lining the hill all the way to the bottom, and on the other side was the mountain going straight up. We prayed as we had never prayed before, knowing we could do nothing to save ourselves. We were in God's hands.

If we jumped, we'd be crushed against the boulders. If we drove into the side of the mountain at this speed, we'd very likely be killed. No brakes on the car and no brakes on the trailer, heading down the mountain faster and faster—when all of a sudden, the car skidded to a stop, although the brake pedal lay useless on the floor.

Immediately, my husband rushed out and blocked the car wheels with large rocks. And there on that mountaintop, we thanked God for sparing our lives, marveling at what had just happened to us, not realizing that this was not the last of the miracles we were to witness.

After inspecting the brakes and realizing there was nothing we could do, we were wondering how we were going to get down off the mountain. Just then, a service car from the station seven miles down in the valley pulled up beside us. The driver said he had just gotten a call that someone was in trouble on the mountaintop. We told him that we hadn't made the call (there was no phone anywhere) but that we were certainly in trouble. After driving around and finding no one else on the entire mountain, he came back and helped us.

Who made that phone call for help? What made the car suddenly stop?

We believe it was God's angels.

Angels must be quick-witted enough to stop imminent collisions in the blink of an eye. Why they don't do it more often is a question we can't answer, but sometimes, even when there's no time to pray . . .

Robert L.'s wife, who lives in Altamonte Springs, Florida, was on her way home with their five- and six-year-olds sitting beside her in the front seat, when a driver to her right decided to turn *left* right in front of her. There wasn't even enough time for Mrs. L. to get her foot off the gas pedal, much less time to apply the brakes.

But the car stopped. Dead still. Completely. No screech, no skidding, no sliding, nothing. The car simply stopped. Not only did the car stop; everything in it stopped too. Neither of the children

177

budged an inch out of their seat. It was as if they were wearing invisible seat belts. This was before seat belts were mandatory for children.

Mrs. L. remembers clearly the screech of brakes behind her as drivers strove valiantly (and successfully) to avoid hitting her. She even remembers the look of horror on the face of the man who had caused the problem when he realized what he was doing. To this day, it is with awe that she remembers that a miracle was performed for her.

God sent Barbara K., of Monroe, Michigan, a "reckless driver" angel to save her from a collision with a real reckless driver. Here is her story:

I was driving home from a baby-sitting job at about 2:00 a. m. with my eight-year-old daughter sleeping in the front seat next to me. Approaching a traffic light, I observed that I was the only car on the road. Stopping for the red light, I suddenly noticed a vehicle in the left-hand turn lane beside me. I thought that was strange at the time, since there had been nobody behind me just seconds earlier, but I dismissed it without thinking anymore about it.

When the light turned green, I accelerated slowly, but suddenly the car next to me sped in front of me, causing me to brake quickly. When I looked up, I couldn't see any sign of the vehicle. The road was straight, so I should have seen taillights.

As I started to accelerate again, I noticed headlights coming fast from my left and suddenly realized that the car was not going to stop! I slammed on my brakes, knocking my daughter off the seat. As the car streaked by, missing me by mere inches, I couldn't determine what color it was because it was traveling at such a high speed. It was then I realized that if the "phantom car" had not cut me off, I would have been in the direct path of that speeding car! I knew instantly that God had sent an angel and even then wondered what purpose God had for my life that He would dramatically prolong it in that way.

By the way, my daughter was fine, just a little shaken up, as I was.

Mrs. Z., of Surrey, British Columbia, never saw anyone at all, but . . . well, how would you explain what happened to her?

I was stopped at a busy intersection, and my car was lifted over to the next lane. I thought, *My goodness, what's happening?* Just then, a car flew past me, going about ninety mph head-on into the lane that I had just occupied. I felt an angel had moved me out of harm's way. Otherwise, I would have surely been killed.

And finally, a story that happened to me (Lonnie), although I was too young to realize what angels did for me at the time: In 1948 my (Lonnie's) parents were traveling to southern California to join the Voice of Prophecy, where Dad was to sing with the King's Heralds quartet. As their car was crossing the desert, little one-year-old me was sleeping on the back seat together with my newest brother Joedy, just a few months old. Dad was driving. The road was a seldom-traveled two-lane. In the distance, an unusual-looking car approached at high speed. As it drew close, Dad could see that a small boat was strapped to the roof upside down.

Just as the approaching car was about to flash by, Dad saw something else. Small whirlwind eddies are not uncommon in the deserts of Nevada and Arizona. These funnel-like clouds can do minor damage to trucks and motor homes if they move across the highway at the wrong time. One of these whirlwinds happened to sweep across the road in front of us at the precise moment when the car with the boat sped past. In a split second the boat was ripped from its moorings, flipped high in the air, and fell directly in front of my parents' speeding automobile.

Dad and Mom hardly had time to realize what was happening, except to utter a prayer that was interrupted in mid-sentence, "Lord, help—"

At that precise instant, the boat lifted itself back up in the air as if with unseen hands, and my parents' car shot past underneath. As Dad looked in his rearview mirror, the boat fell right back down in the exact spot the car had just vacated. Had they hit that boat, I believe there would have been tragedy.

To this day, we believe that an angel picked up that boat at the precise moment of danger and permitted our lives to be spared. My father and his five sons have now given well over a hundred combined years of ministry to the Lord. Praise God! He's in control.

---

1. *Pacific Union Recorder*, 2 November 1987, 2.

CHAPTER

12

More From the Traveler's Aid Logbook

Travel is difficult. It cuts us off from all that is familiar. In fact, the English word *travel* comes from the same Latin root as *travail*, which has to do with torment and suffering. Since travelers face special dangers, they need special protection. Often in lonely places, angels have been the companions of travelers in peril. Those who love God can ask for angels to go with them and protect them from adverse circumstances.

This chapter contains more stories of God's special watch care over His children when they are away from home. The first one is from Jerry D., of Geneva, Switzerland.

In June of 1992, I was traveling with a secular choir that was to do a three-week tour of the former Soviet Union. I and several other Christians in the group purchased Bibles, books, worship music, the movie *Jesus* in Russian, and other material to give away. We had about 350 books in our suitcases. We flew from Boston to New York and were switching airports to fly out of Kennedy Airport, when over the loudspeaker I heard them page our group, mentioning the name of a man whom I didn't know.

I asked our leader if this was a friend of hers. She took the phone call. It was the police in Wenham, Massachusetts, looking for me. They had found my visa for Russia. I didn't know that I didn't have it. The visa itself was in Russian. There was no way they could have tracked me down. They had somehow managed in a few hours to discover the name of the group I was with, the travel agent, the airport, and the time we were going to be in the airport; and they tracked me down within minutes of our departure.

The policeman I talked to had no idea how he had managed to find me.

If I had continued on my journey and arrived in Moscow with no visa and all those Bibles, it could have been disastrous. Was it an angel who called me? Maybe. I picked up a new visa in Finland.

My second story is about the difficulty I had in leaving Russia. Two days before the group's departure, my passport, airline tickets, camera, and some other items were stolen while we were performing. The people in charge of the concert called the militia and the special police. Later that night we saw soldiers questioning people and doing a search of the campground at which we were staying. Everyone in the choir was so upset! Without a passport and airline tickets, it might take weeks of paperwork to get me out of Russia.

Another division of the special police was already aware of our distribution of the religious material and had let me know they were displeased. Everyone asked me if I was scared and what I was going to do. I had prayed and felt as if the Lord had said, "Don't worry; it's all under My control."

One person yelled and screamed at me, "You can't have that attitude now. This is the real world, and this is serious." The Russian police were upset and asked me why I was so cheerful. I told them and everyone, "God knows exactly where my passport, airline tickets, and other things are. If He wants me to have them, He will give them to me. If not, then I will gladly accept being detained in Russia."

The next day we left by bus. On our way to Moscow, we pulled over by a brook to get some water. Fifteen minutes later, another bus pulled up behind us, and out came someone waving my passport and airline tickets. This person said, "A truck forced us off the road; a man got out and gave them to us. He said a man on a motorcycle gave them to him." Everyone was rejoicing.

I thanked the Lord and asked Him, "How about also getting me the rest of my stuff?" A few hours later, we pulled over for lunch. We went to a lake in the woods. After a little while, a special police captain showed up with everything else that had been stolen. This whole time I was telling how God provides and takes care of me. This was an experience that made all these choir members wonder if I didn't have a secret hot line to God. I then took a picture of this special police captain, but as you can most likely guess, it didn't show up on the film, the only one out of twenty-four pictures that didn't turn out.

On November 19, 1966, my mother's boyfriend shot her. The wound would prove fatal some thirty-nine days later. At that time, I was seventeen years old. Our family gave little regard to God or His

Son. My mother lived in Hanover, Pennsylvania, near Gettysburg, and I lived near Pittsburgh, several hundred miles away. The day after my mother was wounded, I bought a bus ticket to York, which was the nearest city to my destination. Because of a severe snowstorm, travel through the Appalachians was treacherous, and our bus arrived in York very late, around one o'clock in the morning.

Once we arrived, I tried to get transportation by cab or bus to Hanover, nineteen miles away, but public transportation was not in service so late at night. I asked around for directions to the local police department and told my story to the desk officer. He confirmed that he had heard of the shooting, and although I was stranded, the police department couldn't help me by providing transportation to Hanover. My only alternative was to wait until 8:00 a.m., at which time I could get public transportation.

The officer did provide a bench for me to rest on until morning. However, the longer I waited, the more desperate I became. All I could think of was that my mother lay dying nineteen miles away and I couldn't get to her.

As I sat in the darkness of the hallway, I felt compelled to leave, to walk, if necessary, all the way to the hospital. The weather was cold ,with six to eight inches of snow on the ground, but I couldn't let that stop me. I remembered having been in York some years before, and I remembered one road in particular that went directly to Hanover. I left the police station through the back door and headed down the street. I was very frightened about being alone, and I knew that nineteen miles would be a long way to walk. But under the circumstances, I felt that I had no choice.

I walked along the berm of the road, with the snow over my tennis shoes and my hands cold and numb from carrying a suitcase.

Slowly, a small car pulled up and stopped. In the car was a young man about twenty years old. He asked me where I was headed. After I told him my story, he instructed me to get in the car. He would make sure I got to the hospital in Hanover. He said he had to stop at his home and leave a note for his mother so she wouldn't worry if she got up in the night and noticed that he hadn't arrived yet.

At his house, he gave me hot chocolate to drink, and then we were on our way. I don't remember any conversation between us from his home to the hospital.

When he dropped me off in front of the hospital, I thanked him for his help and closed the door. I took a few steps, then immediately, I remembered that I should, at the very least, offer him some money for gas. I turned to step back to the car to open the door, but to my surprise, my benefactor and his car were gone. I could see far down the road in both directions, but I could not see him anywhere. At that time, I had no rationale for what happened but just assumed I must be confused by my preoccupation with my mother's condition.

My mother died from her wound on December 25, 1966. Almost three years later, with the faithful witness of friends, I surrendered my life to Christ.

After being a Christian for several years, this incident came to my mind again with crystal clarity. I am as certain as I can be that this was my angel who provided me warmth, kindness, and transportation at a time when no other person would or could provide for a seventeen-year-old crushed beneath the load of tragedy.

I praise God that before I knew Him, He knew me and provided for my needs.

I have been a Christian for the past twenty-four years, and He has never failed to meet me and lift me up; that glory and honor may be given to His name for all things.

—Richard G., Columbus, Ohio.

I arrived in Cologne, Germany, in the winter of 1967, sick with the flu. My bags were scheduled to come on a later train. I was really discouraged and didn't have any money. I had my ticket already in my pocket, and that included the bus ride to the airport in Luxembourg.

I knew I was either going to have to leave my baggage at the train station and go on to Luxembourg or wait and miss the bus to Luxembourg, which would mean I would miss my flight.

I stood in front of a little shop, praying for help. Almost simultaneously, this fellow about my age came up to the window and began to talk. A very friendly person, he listened to my situation and agreed to take me to Luxembourg airport later that night after we had gotten the bags at the train station. Later on, we went to his car, and he introduced me to his brother. Then we went to the train station, got my baggage, and headed for Luxembourg.

We got stuck several times, and it began to snow very heavily in the mountains. At the border, we were in such a rush that we drove right past the guardhouse. The guard came out waving his arms, and my driver put the car in reverse, began to back up, and said, "Give me your passport."

So I handed him my passport, and he handed it to the guard and in a very authoritative way said, "This man is an American, and we're in a hurry to get to the airport."

I've been detained for quite some time at many borders, so I was surprised to hear the guard say, "Oh, by all means, go ahead. Hurry."

At the next guard point, which was manned by Luxembourg officials, we did the same thing. And to my absolute amazement, the guard there said the same thing: "Rush on; hurry and try to get there on time."

By the time we got to Luxembourg, it was too late to catch the plane; we were already nearly an hour late. As we drove up to the airport, my driver rushed out and grabbed the bags, and his brother grabbed some things, and we ran into the airport. And at that moment, we heard one of the engines start up. The plane had been delayed for an hour and five minutes by mechanical problems. At the time, I really didn't think anything of it. I just said, "Goodbye and thank you," and what really occurred to me later, it surely must have been an answer to prayer. And I began to really wonder if it wasn't two angels who were from another time and place, so to speak.

—Skip B.

Jan S., a secretary who used to work near our Voice of Prophecy offices, suspects she once had lunch with an angel. It happened when she was a thirteen-year-old freshman at a boarding academy in Michigan. She had only recently been baptized, and she had never been away from home at all and found the experience somewhat intimidating. The day finally came for her first home leave. To get home, she had to take the Greyhound bus, and to meet the bus she had to have someone take her to the bus station in another town. Well, Murphy's Law took over. Her ride got her there late, and she missed her bus.

Finally, she got on a later bus, but this meant she would have a two-hour layover in Flint, Michigan. At the bus station in Flint, not knowing what to do next, she went to the window and asked for directions. The woman behind the window seemed very busy. "Just sit down over there and listen for your bus number," she said. Jan sat down, then realized she didn't know what that number was. Anxious and scared, she began to cry.

Then a dignified older man came up and sat down beside her. He asked if he could help, and she shared her problem with him. He went up to the window and got all the information that was needed. Then he took Jan to lunch and paid for it. The man sat with her the entire time she had to wait for the bus. His presence soothed and calmed her; there seemed to be a peaceful atmosphere about him. When her bus number was called, he walked her to the bus. She took one step up onto the bus and turned around to thank her benefactor, but he had vanished, though there was nowhere for him to hide.

Bernice D., of Farmington Hills, Michigan, also needed help with public transportation during the Christmas rush. Here's her story:

On December 14, 1976, my husband Ralph died after bypass surgery in Memphis, Tennessee. After making arrangements for his body to be shipped to Flint, Michigan, I returned to our southeast Missouri home to pick up my youngest son, Gary, and begin the journey to Flint, where my older children lived.

We took a small plane from Poplar Bluff, Missouri, to St. Louis, where we changed planes and flew to Chicago. Upon arriving at O'Hare Airport, I was told that Gary and I would have to be on standby, possibly until the next day, because the terminal was crowded with servicepeople going home for Christmas. I turned from the counter with tears in my eyes and prayed, "Jesus, take us home."

A clean-cut young man said to me, "Ma'am, can I help you?"

I said, "I'm trying to get home to my children in Flint to make funeral arrangements for my husband."

He said, "Follow me."

I did so. He took us to a gate. The area was packed. I didn't hear what he said, but the crowd parted, and we walked through the gate to a plane warming up in preparation for taking off. He led us up the stairs, knocked at the door of the plane, and when it was opened, told the flight attendant to give us first-class treatment all the way to Flint. As Gary and I entered the plane, I turned to thank the young man . . . he was gone.

Several years ago, the parents of Anne D. had an encounter with a very special taxi driver. She wrote it out because she believes that relating these experiences helps us to be more aware of the presence of our guardian angels.

My parents migrated to America in 1910. After living in the United States for a time, they took up a homestead in Canada. Farming had its hard times, but it was a wholesome and busy life. The years sped by, and soon Mother and Dad's family was raised, and they were alone again. Then came the time to celebrate their fiftieth wedding anniversary.

My husband and I thought what a special event it might be for them to have a boat ride—they hadn't had one since they had crossed the Atlantic. So we arranged to take them to Seattle, where we boarded one of the *Princess* ferries for Vancouver Island. My husband and I had taken the trip over there several times and always found it such a delightful trip.

On the return trip, we planned to put them on a bus in Spokane, Washington. We had arranged for my sister to meet the bus in Calgary. For some reason, they failed to meet in Calgary. It was about 10:00 p.m. by then, and my parents, not being veteran travelers, felt lost and didn't know what to do.

A bus was about to leave for Edmonton, and it would be going through Lacombe, their hometown, so that seemed to them the best route to go. When they arrived in Lacombe, my dad asked the bus driver if he would mind letting them get off the bus four miles out of Lacombe, which would put them on the corner near their home. It was far past midnight by then, and they were weary travelers after such a long day.

Before Dad realized it, the bus was beyond their corner about two miles. When Dad told the driver that their corner had been missed, he pulled off on the side of the road, no doubt feeling bad that the elderly couple with their heavy suitcase would be hard put to trudge back two miles in the wee hours of the morning. Just then, the bus driver noticed a car parked by the side of the road, just where they had stopped.

With a sudden idea, he said to Dad, "Let me ask the driver of this car if he would take you back to your home." The driver was very willing. He drove my parents right to their door and helped them unload their suitcase. Dad turned to get his billfold out of his pocket to pay the man for his kindness, but when he looked up, there was no man and no car. He never even heard a car take off! Surely the Lord had sent an angel to help two weary travelers.

Was it a dream, a strong impression, or had someone spoken in the still of the night? Whatever, it had awakened me from a sound sleep. Gordon was in danger, of that I was certain, and I must pray. Hastily I slipped out of my bed and knelt to pray that the Lord would protect my husband as he traveled the mountain roads at such a late hour.

The boys' junior camp was in progress at McCall, Idaho. Ministerial interns helped as counselors, something my husband enjoyed doing.

So I was more than surprised when Gordon returned home several days early, toting three little fellows who had attended camp from our district. He explained that he had to get them home that night. They had suffered such homesickness that he didn't want them enduring another night away from home. Their sad faces affirmed his decision. After a late and hasty supper, they were on their way—two boys to Long Creek and the other boy to Hamilton—

a round trip of 106 miles through the mountains.

It would be late before Gordon would come home. Our children were asleep, and I, too, retired. I must have slept a good two hours or more before being awakened. But after praying earnestly for God's protecting care over my weary husband, I again crawled into bed and fell asleep. It must have been a light sleep, for I soon heard the car pulling into our detached garage. I awaited the familiar footsteps and the sound of the key in the latch. But there was only silence.

Had I been mistaken? I lay awake, listening and hoping, but nothing. God had heard my prayer, of that I was certain, so I relaxed and again fell asleep. Then after what seemed a long while, I heard those welcome sounds. "Thank You, Lord," I breathed.

"It's taken you a long time," I said as Gordon came to bed. "I thought I heard you pull in some time ago."

"I did, but I've been sleeping in the garage," he explained. "Actually, I have no idea how I got here. I just don't remember anything from the town of Mt. Vernon eight miles away until opening my eyes as I pulled into the garage. Then I was sleeping so soundly that I just continued sleeping until I could wake up enough to get into the house."

Such a wonderful heavenly Father, who in answer to my prayer graciously allowed the guardian angel of my tired husband to finish the last lap of the journey home. God is good and our angels so kind.

—Nan H., Scottsdale, Arizona.

Very few people have the privilege of having an extended conversation with an angel. Martin M., of Highland, California, sent us a remarkable story that he had never shared with anyone outside his close family.

In 1962, having just reenlisted for a second tour of duty with the regular U.S. Army, I was assigned to Fort Ord, California, where I received orders to report to Brooklyn Naval Yard to board a ship for Germany and duty with the 7th Army.

My immediate interest before reporting to New York City was to first drive to Connecticut and marry my fiancée, who had agreed to meet me in Europe once I made arrangements with the army.

On a bright January morning, I pointed my car east. My intention was to drive straight through to Connecticut, get married, and then report to the Brooklyn Naval Yard.

Having driven nonstop to Illinois, I stopped at a turnpike gas station sometime after midnight. After filling the tank, I felt the overpowering need to shut my eyes for a few minutes. Parking the car between two eighteen-wheelers, I laid my head down on the front seat. Then the strangest thing occurred—a man suddenly appeared in my car and began telling me about God and the glory of God.

That very normal-appearing, middle-aged man was wearing a tan shirt and pants. I distinctly recall him telling me of the beauty and glory of God and His wondrous kingdom and the many things that awaited God's children.

It seemed that hours passed while this individual continued to talk. Although the years have erased part of my memory, the central theme was the description of heaven in words that defy human understanding. Not once did my visitor deviate from the focus of heaven and God. Moreover, he kept telling me not to worry and to lay my head on his lap and sleep, which I did.

After these many years, I cannot recall just where the truck stop was located, but it was many miles from the Indiana border.

The final episode was, and is, hard to believe. When I awoke, I was sitting in the driving position, on the turnpike, with the sun just coming up in the east and the Indiana border racing into view.

I recall turning to the passenger side to talk to my new companion and discovering that he was no longer present. I vividly realized that my visitor had been no ordinary being, and I believed then, as I still do, that my friend was my guardian angel. I believe that God permitted me to become acquainted with the very angel assigned to watch over me.

I also realized that I was no longer tired. For the remainder of the trip, and well after arriving in Connecticut, I was as alert and energetic as when speeding over the Indiana border. Imagine heaven, where we will no longer experience tiredness and stress.

The wonder of it all. Upon awaking, my senses were entirely on God. I was surrounded with His glory and presence. For the balance of my trip, I did nothing but sing to the Lord.

No words can possibly convey that experience. This was not a dream or psychological fantasy. Only God, His angel, and myself are certain. I only wish every Christian could enjoy what our Lord allowed a tired and lonely twenty-year-old to witness.

Rest assured, friend, your guardian angel never sleeps.

Although most angels don't stay around for a conversation, they often speak invisibly to God's children in terse voices, warning of danger. Angels are often heard and not seen.

Mary F., of Lawai, Hawaii, and her husband escaped death on the highway twice while working as literature evangelists. The first time, they were calling on interests in the area of Palmer, Massachusetts. As they approached an overpass, Mary heard a voice suggesting that they turn the car around and go back to the last house they had visited—a house where no one had been home moments before. Just as they turned around, they heard a terrible crash. A large laundry truck had crashed through the guard rail on the overpass, landing in the very spot where they would have been had they not heeded God's voice.

After they saw to it that the injured truck driver was taken to the hospital, they returned to that last house. Still, no one was home.

Mary's second "near-death experience" on the road occurred on a Sunday near Westfield, Massachusetts. The Lord had been blessing their work lately, and that afternoon, Mary was so eager to get out of the car that she almost forgot to stop and pray. Her husband stopped her and said, "Wait a second. Let's pray." He had parked the car on the wrong side of the street, and she had left her car door slightly ajar. Suddenly, a car driven by a teenager without a license (as they later discovered) raced by at full speed, ripping the door from the car.

They hadn't even had time to pray when this happened. If Mary's husband had not stopped her from getting out of the car, she would have been right in the path of the oncoming car. Mary decided that it always pays to pray, and she never again left the car to enter a home without a prayer.

That same inner voice saved Cerrell S., of Walla Walla, Washington, from tragedy on the road.

I, too, have believed there have been angels in my life, guiding and helping me. One incident I'll never forget happened when my daughter was only four years old. We were not wearing our seat belts in our little Volkswagen convertible. We were on our usual route down to the grocery store through a residential area. The stoplight at the corner by the store had just turned green, and I was ready to drive right through the intersection.

A voice inside me was emphatically saying, "Stop!" That totally violated my natural instincts; my mind was on the green light, grocery shopping, and so forth. But the message was so strong that I applied the brakes. At that moment, a large car sped from my daughter's side through the intersection, running the red light. It would have been at the exact time we would have been in the center of the intersection. I estimated that the car was probably going at least fifty miles per hour.

I just said, "Thank You, Jesus!" We would not have been here today had it not been for Him.

Ruth E., of Harvest, Alabama, was driving through a parking lot looking for a parking space one day. She had just turned right after stopping for a stop sign, when she was asked (in her mind), "What would you do if you saw a car speeding toward you?"

She thought, *I'd get off the gas, get on the brake, and blow my horn.*

"All right," said the inner voice. "Get off your gas, get on your brake, and blow your horn."

Immediately, she saw a car speeding toward her. It would have smashed into her passenger side if she had not been warned. Though she was all alone in the car, she sensed a presence beside her and thanked God.

Michael J., of Lexington, Kentucky, was delivered from danger by the voice of an angel in the summer of 1985.

I was driving to a college in Texas for summer school. I became tired and pulled into a rest area. I lay down in the front seat of my car and planned on sleeping for about four hours. After about only one hour, I found myself suddenly wide awake, apparently for no reason. Then I heard a masculine voice speaking to me. This voice seemed to have no inflection, yet sounded melodious. Although he spoke in a normal volume, I got the impression that to him it was a hushed whisper. He said, "You're in danger; sit up, and everything will be all right." As I wondered what kind of danger I could be in, I felt compelled to obey his command. When I sat up, I immediately understood. There was no one else in the rest area except for myself and one other man, who had parked his car about fifty yards away. He was walking straight for my car, looking down at the ground and smiling to himself. When he finally looked up, he saw me staring at him and suddenly became frightened. He then flipped around 180 degrees and ran as fast as he could to his car.

God cares. When we are distressed, He is distressed. He is a helper of the helpless. When we call upon Him, He answers. He doesn't always, or even usually, answer in such a remarkable and miraculous way. But now and then, just to let us know He's watching, He does.

CHAPTER

13

Warning Voices, Wooing Voices

Whenever possible, angels seem to prefer to be heard and not seen, as befits messengers. "Messenger" is the meaning of the Greek and Hebrew words usually translated "angel" in the Bible, although *emissary* perhaps conveys the full meaning of these words better. In over half of the angel appearances described in the Bible, angels appear as messengers.

Angels bring messages from God in different ways to different people. Angels appeared to Joseph, the husband of Mary, only in dreams (see Matthew 1:20; 2:13,

19). Yet they apparently appeared in person to Zechariah (see Luke 1:11-13), to Mary (verses 26-38), and to the shepherds in the field at the birth of Jesus (see Luke 2:9-14). They often appeared to the prophets in visions, in which they served as guides and teachers.

A few years ago, Harold Luccock pointed out in the *Christian Century* that, according to his tongue-in-cheek research, whenever angels have a message to bring to someone in the Bible, it's quite often a variation on "Get up, and get going!" An angel comes to Peter in jail and says, "Rise quickly." An angel says to Gideon, "Arise and go in this thy might." An angel says to Elijah, "Arise and eat." An angel appears to Joseph in a dream, when Herod is about to slaughter the infants, and says, "Go quickly." An angel appears to Philip and says, "Arise and go." Really, the angels are monotonous talkers, says Luccock. They always say the same thing: "Arise, hurry!"

The angels in the following stories, then, are right in character with their biblical counterparts, because they involve people in danger who needed to wake up.

Barbara N., of Huntsville, Alabama, stayed up late one night to watch the late movie. Her older sister and her three boys had gone to bed and were in a deep sleep.

I had become hungry and decided to boil some eggs. I then went to the den to finish watching the movie and soon fell asleep, with the eggs still boiling. As you can see, our lives were in great danger.

All of a sudden, I heard someone calling my name. I woke up and heard the voice one more time, very clearly. Then I noticed smoke throughout the house. I just jumped up and ran to the kitchen and removed the burning pot from the stove. I then opened the windows and ran from room to room, only to find that everyone was still asleep. I stood over my sister and asked her if she had called me, but she was still in a deep sleep. I went back to the den a little bit afraid that an angel had called my name to save our lives. I bowed on my knees and prayed a prayer of thanks to God.

About midmorning, Dr. Roscoe S., of Riverside, California, was sitting in his office on the La Sierra campus of Loma Linda University, when he suddenly had a strong urge to go to his house to get something that he had planned to take with him that morning, but had forgotten. As he thought about it later, he realized that whatever it was could just as well have waited until noon, when he would be going to the house for lunch anyway. But the urge was so strong that he immediately went to the car, drove to the house, retrieved the material, and started back to his car.

However, as he was passing the dining room, he heard a voice—a "silent" voice inside his head, but the message was very clear: "As long as you're here, why not look in the garage?"

Dr. S. knew of no reason why he should look in the garage. But that was not the first time he had heard that voice, and he knew that there must be a good reason to look in the garage and that if he didn't, he would be sorry. So instantly he turned and walked through the dining room and kitchen, opened the door to the attached garage, and stuck his head in.

He was astonished to see flames in one corner leaping about eighteen inches into the air. He ran to the kitchen sink, picked up a pan he found there with water in it, rushed back, and threw it onto the fire. The flames promptly went out. Then his attention was drawn to other flames behind the washing machine and the dryer, creeping up the wall. *This must be bigger than I first thought,* he decided. *I had better call the fire department.*

He started for the phone. On the way he passed the broom closet, inside of which he kept a home fire extinguisher. "I guess I can take time for that," he said to himself and jerked the extinguisher off its mount. (Fire officials strongly recommend that in situations like this, one should call the fire department first, then attempt to extinguish the flames.)

The fire extinguisher was soon empty, and the fire was out. And the still, small voice had averted another tragedy.

Often God communicates His will through a voice. Sometimes the voice of God sounds like thunder, sometimes like the sound of many waters, and sometimes like a trumpet. But sometimes it is the "still, small voice" that Elijah heard in the desert (see 1 Kings 19:11-13), warning against danger or beckoning to repentance. Angels are far more interested in waking people up spiritually than they are in waking them out of physical sleep, for the fires of hell are a far greater danger than any house fire.

God promised His people that His Spirit would guide those who were willing to listen:

> O people of Zion, who live in Jerusalem, you will weep no more. How gracious he will be when you cry for help! As soon as he hears, he will answer you. Although the Lord gives you the bread of adversity and the water of affliction, your teachers will be hidden no more; with your own eyes you will see them. Whether you turn to the right or to the left, your ears will hear a voice behind you, saying, "This is the way; walk in it" (Isaiah 30:19-21).

> My sheep listen to my voice; I know them, and they follow me (John 10:27).

It was a vision and a voice that changed Paul's life (see Acts 22:7-9; 26:14). That voice still speaks today; it is still changing lives.

Here I am! I stand at the door and knock. If anyone hears my voice and opens the door, I will come in and eat with him, and he with me (Revelation 3:20).

Today, if you hear his voice, do not harden your hearts as you did in the rebellion (Hebrews 3:15).

I (Tim) heard the late Josephine Cunnington Edwards tell this story at the church where I was pastoring, and I asked her permission to write it down.

Josephine grew up with quite a few brothers, but Bill was the wild one in the family. As a boy he refused to be baptized. For fifty years he smoked, drank, and swore up a storm.

Bill wasn't a harsh, evil person. He was kind to animals and gentle to old people. He was honest. He didn't lie or steal, as far as Josephine knew. But he had had some misfortune in his life. Once, a jealous man at a party beat him up and left a hole in his face under one eye. Partly because of the troubles he had been through, Bill wanted nothing to do with God.

While Josephine was serving as a missionary in Africa, she devoted every Thursday as a day of fasting and prayer for Bill.

Around 1951, Bill's wife Mary learned that she had terminal cancer. During one of their regular weekly prayer services, the Voice of Prophecy staff prayed for her, and she was miraculously healed. After that, she became the head deaconess in a church in Tampa, Florida.

Sometime in the early sixties, Josephine led out in the Week of Prayer at a small church in Athens, Alabama. She asked the group to pray for Bill. They began with a consecration service in which they confessed sin and came into one accord.

Then a man named Frank jumped up and asked the folks to pray for his wife, who had terminal heart disease. Everyone, even the children, prayed. In answer to those prayers, the woman was healed.

The next week, Josephine received a letter from Mary. Mary had come home from church one day to find Bill throwing all of his tobacco into the wastebasket, saying, "I'm never going to touch it again." Then he poured his liquor down the drain. Josephine's prayers became more fervent. "You've gone so far, Lord; now take him all the way."

A few months later, Josephine moved to Idaho to teach at Gem State Academy. She had not gotten completely unpacked when Mary called her up. "Josephine," she said, "are you doing something special out there?"

"Yes," she replied, "I've been praying."

Mary burst into tears. "The Lord has answered our prayer." Here is how it happened:

One day Mary heard Bill make a funny noise and stepped over to find his face bathed in tears. "Bill," she cried, "what's the matter?"

He couldn't talk for a while. Finally, he said, "Go call the pastor, and I will tell you while he is coming."

Finally, Bill was able to talk. "I was just sitting here reading," he said, "when I heard the door open behind me. I turned around, and—oh, Mary, it was the Lord! I knew Him by the nail prints in His hands. No picture can ever portray the love in His eyes. Mary, if you saw the Lord, you could never refuse Him anything He asked.

"He said, 'Bill, I have a special request to make of you. I have fifty years of prayer for you to answer for. Your parents went to their graves believing that they would never see you in the kingdom. Bill, I would love to have a grand surprise for them when they get to heaven. Won't you give your life to Me, so that I can present you to them there?' "

Shortly afterward, Bill was baptized. One glimpse of that face was enough to change the course of a lifetime.

No doubt that was a noisy day for the angels, for "there is

rejoicing in the presence of the angels of God over one sinner who repents" (Luke 15:10).

The next two stories also involve the Voice of Prophecy. The first one comes to us from Chester L., of Wheelersburg, Ohio. One Saturday morning in 1951, Chester was home alone. His family had gone away for the day, and he was lying down on the davenport just thinking about things. He had not been going to church or studying the Bible much.

All of a sudden, a voice spoke to him, saying, "Do you have enough of the Word of God in your heart?"

He sat up and looked around and saw that no one was nearby. He believed right away that it was either an angel or the Lord Himself who had spoken to him, no doubt warning him that he was not doing right by neglecting church attendance and Bible study.

Chester wasted no time. He wrote to the Voice of Prophecy and asked for our Bible-study course. Today, Chester still listens to the broadcast.

The second story is from Josephine R., of Simi Valley, California. In the fall of 1971, she had an accident in her home. This necessitated a visit to the emergency room at the Simi Valley Adventist Hospital, not far from our Voice of Prophecy studios.

In the waiting room, she picked up one of our Bible-study request cards, filled it out, and sent it in.

Soon the course arrived in the mail. After a year of study, baptism was suggested. Josephine was not sure this was God's plan for her, so she prayed for several months, asking for an answer.

One night she suddenly awoke, sitting straight up. There was a glowing haze in the room, blocking out everything except a scroll held by two fingers.

On the scroll was inscribed John 14:16: "I will pray the Father, and he shall give you another Comforter, that he may abide with you for ever" (KJV).

Josephine knew this was the answer to her prayer. She was baptized on February 24, 1973.

One evening in 1975, I was driving around alone. I had attempted suicide twice, weeks before. My wife had left me, and I didn't want to live. I wanted help, but it seemed like there was no way out.

I stopped at a coffee shop about three o'clock in the morning. There was a younger man sitting at the counter, so I went and sat next to him. It didn't take long for us to start talking. He seemed worse off than I. I then started telling him about the love of Jesus, His purpose, His life, His death, and His resurrection. The more we talked, the better I felt.

It was about five in the morning by now, and something told me that if I was ever going to accept Jesus Christ into my life, I had to do it before the sun came up.

I went to my car and humbly talked to Jesus. When I opened my eyes, I saw a form come down from heaven, right before my eyes. I invited this angelic form to come into me, and he did. I felt him come into my body. It was like he took my heart, like a sponge, and wrung out all the hurt. I felt so happy—there was no more sadness in my heart.

I felt the angel leave my body. I begged and pleaded for him not to leave me, because with him here, everything would be all right. He said he had to go, that there were many more people he had to see before the sun came up. I was crying.

Later I doubted what had happened. In 1988 when I was

studying the Bible, I read that almost the same had happened to Jacob. I am now a Seventh-day Adventist Christian.

−Wayne P., Lewisville, Texas.

I was a drug dealer for approximately seven years, although I had been reared in the church. My grandfather was the pastor.

One day I realized that this was not what my mother raised me to do, and I looked in the mirror and acknowledged that I was not a good man in God's eyesight because I was not even good in my own sight. So I cried and asked God to make me into a good man.

God was silent.

Christmas Eve 1979 came, and I proceeded to deliver my merchandise to eagerly waiting customers.

Early Christmas morning found me in an after-hours joint with a fellow drug dealer. Then without warning, something strange began to occur on the inside of me. Because I had a fearsome reputation to uphold, I dared not tell my partner of the strange, yet wonderful change I was going through, for I was also affiliated with the Mafia at the time.

My associate eventually took me home. It was a silent trip. Finally, he broke out and said, "You know what, Geno? God is in the air!"

"You're right!" I replied.

An old man began crossing the street in front of us, and he stopped and seemed to look right at me, and my partner said, "That could be God right there, and we wouldn't even know it."

"You're right!" I said again.

Suddenly, I was no longer in the car, but I was standing on a pure, white, sparkling road that went straight down the center of a crystal sea.

IN THE PRESENCE OF ANGELS

It was made known to me that I was in "heaven." As a matter of fact, any question I would have normally asked was just simply made known to me.

The Lord appeared in the form of a great white-yellow light, and since I had no questions, I just simply said, "Lord, let me stay!"

The Lord replied, "You must go back into the world from which you came and find My lost sheep."

I tried to plead with Him to let me stay, for I knew I was where I wanted to be forever, so I pleaded, "But, Lord." But immediately I was back in the car with my partner. He was still talking as if I never had left.

I interrupted him and told him that something very wonderful was happening, but I couldn't explain it right now. I invited him to come over the next day, because I wanted him to be a part of it.

I went upstairs and lay down. The Holy Spirit touched me on my left brow, and I went into a deep sleep, yet I was still able to see myself.

An angel came into my room bearing a silver pitcher and with that pitcher poured wisdom into me through my head. The angel left. The Holy Spirit touched me again, and I awoke.

It was then for the first time that I understood what had happened. Astonished, I rose to my knees in the middle of my bed, stretched out my arms, and said, "Good Lord! I've been born again!" Amen.

—Eugene H., Cincinnati, Ohio.

This letter is in response to your request of real-life encounters with angelic beings. My name is Tony. I'm married with three children and operate a painting business in Placerville, a small town in northern California. I had such an experience sixteen years ago, the day I became born again.

Please bear with me as I try to explain a few significant events that I believe led to this encounter.

I was raised in a home in which both parents and all of my brothers and sisters used drugs and relished the "partying" lifestyle. I resented them deeply for this. I refused to participate in their way of life and was very proud of myself. I heard the gospel for the first time when I was sixteen.

The person who shared the gospel with me was extremely thorough. He was a very zealous new convert, who now pastors a church here in Placerville. His name is John Cowper, a great-grandnephew of the poet William Cowper, who penned the famous verse "God moves in mysterious ways, His wonders to perform. He plants His feet beneath the sea and rides upon the storm."

John and I worked together in a restaurant, and he would share with me daily, beginning with scriptural reasons for believing in God, fulfilled prophecy, and the atoning work of Christ. I remember what he stressed most was how all people were naturally bound in darkness, and if they would confess to the Lord Jesus Christ, they would "step into the light," and all things would become new. This was his experience, and he wanted desperately for me and others to share it.

I went to church with him a few times and asked Jesus into my heart, but the light and joy never came. John was patient with me and had all the answers to my many fears, excuses, and doubts. Still, the "light" never went on.

One day John discovered the scripture concerning "turning one over to Satan for the destruction of the flesh" and shared it with me. He told me he was praying this prayer just for me. I really didn't mind. Deep down, I wanted to believe the way he believed. Soon John took another job, and my life took a radical change for the worse—toward the very things I had resented in my family members.

By the time I turned seventeen, I had become a drug abuser.

IN THE PRESENCE OF ANGELS

Just weeks after my eighteenth birthday, I stole money from an employer and found myself in the county jail. Two years earlier, I had contempt for the kind of person I had now become. My life was in the gutter, and I was feeling terrible about it. I wanted desperately to change.

Very soon after getting out of jail, I met a young woman whom I fell in love with at first sight. She seemed so virtuous and happy. I was extremely concerned about what she would think of me when she learned that I had just gotten out of jail. I decided to tell her on our second date. I was completely unprepared for her response. She said, "I forgive you, because I'm a Christian."

My mind raced back to the times when John had witnessed to me. Her words were echoing in my ears as if God was speaking them Himself. Suddenly, I felt the burning conviction of sin and His complete forgiveness. I began to cry. With my eyes closed, I turned my face from hers.

With my face still turned away, I opened my eyes. In front of me, suspended several feet off the ground, I saw a pair of feet. They had sandals on them. They weren't normal feet. They seemed to be made of light. They were translucent white, and they seemed to glow. The sandals were white too. I could see the hem of a garment, and I looked up quickly.

As quickly as I could comprehend what I was seeing, I began to question. And as the being disappeared, I saw a flowing white robe and a sash. The light that came from them was dazzling. I could see forearms extending outward from the midst of all the light. I saw a face made of the same dazzling white light. His face was long and slender. He had a high forehead and a large nose. His hair seemed to touch his shoulders, and I could almost see a beard.

There was so much light coming from him that the perimeter of his body was fuzzy. Only his eyes were different. They were a sparkling amber yellow, and they looked right at me. His face showed little expression. It seemed very firm and confident.

I know that the young woman next to me saw nothing. If it

was Jesus Himself, or an angel, I cannot say with certainty. I can only say that since that moment, I have tried to live for Jesus.
—Tony G., Placerville, California.

My name is Rachel J. I live in Anaheim, California, and I'm fifteen years old. A year ago I was a very rebellious girl. I was very coldhearted and never cared about other people's feelings. Finally, around April, I got pregnant.

The thought of abortion never crossed my mind because when I was ten years old, I saw a special on abortion. Since then, I promised myself that if I ever got pregnant by accident, I would never do that to the baby. My decision would be between putting the baby up for adoption or keeping the baby.

Around October I fell asleep on the chair, and I felt some kind of shock run through my body. I awoke very frightened. An hour later, my mom came home, and I hesitantly asked her if she could buy me a Bible.

That night, I read my Bible for a while, then put it down when I started to get sleepy. Then I saw a light go on in the hall and thought it was my mom coming into my bedroom. I heard her start reading Matthew 7:7-12. I liked what I heard: "Seek and you shall find . . ."

The next day I asked my mom if she was having trouble sleeping, and she said, "No, why?"

"Because I heard you reading my Bible."

She said she had come into my room, but just to give my sister her medicine. But the strange thing was, that night I had just finished reading that chapter, and even though I had read it through, it didn't stick in my mind.

The next night, I went to bed, but when I felt someone watching me, I opened my eyes and saw a shape that looked like my mom

209

sitting at the side of my bed. She told me to help my mom with everything. She told me not to be afraid for my mom because she was watching her, and has been ever since my mom was a little girl. She also said in times of trouble, always seek the Lord.

A week after I had my baby, I accepted the Lord into my life. My mom has rededicated her life to the Lord too.

I just pray that everyone out there will just realize that what they're doing isn't fun; it's evil. The really fun thing is having Christ in your life and knowing that every day that passes is one day closer to Jesus' coming. God bless you!

Sometimes in their desire to save as many people as possible, angels even invite people to church—it happened to Tobey H., of Bridgman, Michigan.

Tobey was brought up a Lutheran, as that is the state church in Norway, where he was born. He married a German woman whom he met in the U.S. She was a Catholic. Neither of them practiced their religion. Tobey's wife died in 1976, so when Lucille met him, he was a widower.

Lucille was attending Mission Institute at Andrews University in the summer of 1977 in preparation for mission service in Brazil. One day she saw a sign on the bulletin board saying, "Blueberries. U-pick at Tobey's!" Lucille loved blueberries, so she and a friend went to Tobey's.

Tobey showed them to his blueberry patch, and as they talked and picked, he picked too. And he kept putting *his* blueberries into *their* buckets! With his help, the buckets were soon full. Before Lucille left, Tobey found out that she and her friend were leaving soon for the mission field, so he asked them to write him when they arrived.

Two weeks later, Tobey was down in his blueberry house

straightening up for the day, when he glanced up and saw a car drive in. A man got out and headed straight for the blueberry house.

Tobey went out to greet him. "Do you have blueberries?" he asked. "I'd like to pick some."

"Why, yes," Tobey said, and took him out into the patch and got him started. Then Tobey went back to the berry house.

About half an hour later, the man came back with his containers full and said, "You have nice berries. How much do I owe you?"

Tobey said, "You're the first customer of the day, so there's no charge." Tobey assumed he would then be on his way, but he walked right into the berry house and sat down, so Tobey followed him in and sat down too.

At first, the man didn't say anything, but then he commented, "You know quite a few people from Andrews University, don't you?"

"Yes, I do. They are my main customers."

"That's good. How do you like these people?"

"I like them very much. I've noticed they are always so helpful and willing to lend a hand when needed."

Then the stranger asked, "What do you think of their religion?"

"Well, to tell you the truth, I don't know too much about their religion, but they are very friendly and happy people. It must be a good religion."

As they sat there talking, Tobey had a feeling that the man wasn't looking at him—he was looking *through* him. He glanced back to see if there was someone behind him, but there wasn't.

Then the man asked, "Would you like to know more about their religion?"

Tobey was quiet for a moment, thinking about the two women who had visited him just a week or so before. "Why, yes," he said.

"That's fine," the strange visitor remarked, and he got up, walked out, and headed for his car.

Tobey sat there for a moment, trying to understand the strange questions. Then he hurried out and called after the man, shouting, "Say, mister, where are you from? Who are you?"

The man turned his head and with a faint smile on his lips answered, "Just a friend. Just a friend," and went on.

Tobey went back into the berry house and looked out the window toward his house to watch the stranger leave in his car. But there was no man . . . and there was no car!

"That's very strange!" he said to himself, and he sat down to try to figure it all out. Besides, there were the blueberries the man had picked. He had left them right there on the table!

One morning about two weeks after this experience with the strange man, two men came to his door. They were from Andrews University and wondered if they could study the Bible with him.

He invited them in, saying, "Yes, I've been expecting you!"

They were surprised at this remark, and Tobey was surprised too! But right then and there, they had their first Bible study together, and every week after that, they met at his place to search the Word.

One of the men who gave the studies was Mr. Fred Dyer. He asked Tobey, "Have you ever been to the Seventh-day Adventist church?"

Tobey said, "I have been there, but I have never gone inside. I thought it was just for the students and professors there at the university."

Mr. Dyer then said, "Well, Tobey, you know it says right over the front door of the church, 'This is a House of Prayer for *all* people.' That means you too!"

So Tobey went to church the next week with Mr. and Mrs. Dyer . . . and the next . . . and the next. Each time they would insist on his staying for dinner.

One Sabbath afternoon, after the delicious dinner, they were in the living room, and Mr. Dyer said, "Tobey, you have been so quiet. Is there something on your mind? Is something bothering you?"

Tobey then told him all about the mysterious appearance and disappearance of the man who came that day to pick blueberries. He told Fred that he had gone to the church the next week after his strange visit and waited outside the front entrance to see if he could see the man again. No luck. The next week it was the same story at another entrance to the church.

They discussed the matter and decided it must have been Tobey's guardian angel.

After a year of Bible studies, Tobey was baptized in this very church. He and Lucille carried on a correspondence while she was in the mission field, and this eventually led to marriage. Tobey still hasn't seen that mysterious "man" again, but he is happy to think that he must have met his very own guardian angel. And he is looking forward to meeting him again someday.

For the last two thousand years, there has been a great deal of speculation as to the identity of the star that led the wise men to the Baby Jesus, as recorded in Matthew 2. Books have been written suggesting various celestial phenomena that the Magi might have seen.

All of this effort is wasted, for it is quite impossible for any astronomical object to stand over a particular town and indicate a particular house in that town (see Matthew 2:9). That "star" was more likely a group of angels celebrating the birth of Christ.

A similar miracle occurred on January 1, 1990, when a very bright light broke up a beer party and led the people to the site of an Adventist Youth campfire.

In the district of Nagwengwere, Malawi, near Malamulo Mission Hospital, two Adventist Youth groups decided to join together for a campfire meeting on New Year's Day. About 130 people had arrived at the site by 2:30 p.m. They began the meeting with songs, verses, stories, and dramas. Toward evening, when they were preparing to light the campfire, a torrential downpour drenched them and threatened to make a campfire impossible. But when they checked the wood they had prepared for the fire, they were surprised to find that it was still dry.

As dusk drew on, they lighted the fire and gathered around to enjoy its warmth and to dry their clothes. They were just beginning to enjoy an evening of songs and fellowship when some very loud music from a nearby beer party began to destroy the peace and quiet of their campfire atmosphere.

Then suddenly the loud party music ceased, and very shortly thereafter, two women came running into the light of the campfire, all out of breath. "If it's time to go to heaven, or if it's the end of the world, we want to be here with you!" they exclaimed

When one of the young people questioned their excitement, they explained what had happened at the beer party. A great big shining star, brighter than a full moon, had appeared in the night sky above their drinking place and started to move away from them down to where the Adventist Youth were having their campfire. When it arrived over the campfire, it stayed there in the sky for ten or fifteen minutes. The whole village saw it, and, of course, were so amazed and frightened that all thoughts of partying were dismissed from their minds.

Many of the villagers have become interested in finding out more about what the youth at the campfire were doing. They feel this great light in the sky, like the star over Bethlehem, was sent to guide them to something very important.

The youth who were at the campfire believe that even though they didn't see the light hovering over them, God is using their campfire to bring the light of God's love and salvation to people whose lives have been hidden in darkness.

—T. L. Temani, as told by Leonard Atkins, Blantyre, Malawi, Africa.

CHAPTER

14

Helpers

of

Many Hues

So far, most of the angels in this book have appeared as men—usually blond. Why does it seem that angels always appear as white males? Well, they don't—not always. It depends on the time, the place, and sometimes the ethnic identity of the person in need. We have saved for this chapter most of the stories in which the angel takes on the appearance of a woman or a person of color.

Hair was the only thing white on the angel Lawrence P. of Fort Smith, Arkansas, met. Here is Larry's letter:

While growing up in California, I was one of four children, and we were quite poor. For each of us kids, real joy was eating a hot meal together or watching Mother divide a candy bar between the four of us. Conditions were so bad inside our remote country home that I was afraid of taking a bath, because I'd returned home one afternoon to discover that a black widow spider had taken up her residence inside the tub!

We were the poorest of the poor, but we had love for God and each other. Mother always taught us the importance of prayer, Bible reading, and church attendance. Both parents relied on a higher power to see us through life's struggles.

When my dad lost his job at E. C. Loomis and Sons, we were penniless, left on the verge of hunger. Mother prayed for God's divine intervention. Knowing there was nothing left in the house to eat, she feared we would starve. Dad nervously pondered what he should do. And when all else failed, he, too, prayed.

The answer to prayer came in a recurring thought that played over and over in his mind, telling him to get in the car and drive north to San Luis Obispo. Not knowing anyone in that city, Dad tried to dismiss it as imagination, but the thought refused to leave his mind. Finally, Dad told Mother he was going to San Luis Obispo.

"But, Dick," Mother retorted keenly. "You don't know anybody in San Luis, and furthermore, you might not get halfway there before you run out of gas."

"I know." Dad shrugged as he walked toward the door.

"I'll be praying for you," Mother said with a smile.

"Thanks, I'll need it."

With those words, my father walked to the green Ford station wagon and drove to San Luis Obispo. All the way there, the gas gauge stayed near empty. Like Abraham of old, my father followed God's gentle leading, venturing to a place where he was a stranger.

Three hours had passed when, gazing out the window, I caught a glimpse of the green car turn into our driveway from the country road. I dashed out the door to meet the car as it coasted to a stop. Oddly enough, Dad was grinning—he had been frowning when he left. I hurried forward to see what he was so happy about, and that's when I noticed the groceries in the back seat. Mother came out to meet Dad, and she, too, noticed the groceries. By the look in her eyes, she was a bit suspicious.

"Dick, where did you get these groceries?"

"Now, Mother, everything's going to be all right."

"Dick, what have you done?"

"Now, Mother . . ."

"Dick, you didn't . . ."

"No."

"Then tell me where and how did you get these groceries!"

"All right, you and the kids come inside, and while we put away the food, I'll tell you all about it."

Eagerly we followed Dad into the kitchen, where he told us of his experience of being visited by some divine providence that he could not explain.

In the first place, he told us that he felt scared and all alone when he entered San Luis Obispo. Once inside the city, he felt strangely drawn toward the city park, where he drove down a side street and parked the car against the curb. Looking up, he saw the park grocery store. Realizing he was broke, he wondered why he had stopped so close to what his family needed most— food. He waited for a while, but nothing happened.

Did I act in haste? he asked himself. *Did I make a big mistake by coming here today, or should I have stayed at home with the wife and kids?*

As he stepped from the car, he looked up and saw a white-haired black man standing near him on the sidewalk, neatly dressed in bib overalls. The humble servant walked over to my father and said that he understood my dad's troubles and wanted to help. My father exclaimed that there was some mistake, as he had never seen the man before in his life. The man smiled and said, "Just come with me."

Soon my father and the man were inside the grocery store.

IN THE PRESENCE OF ANGELS

The stranger asked the clerk for a cardboard box that had been trimmed neatly with a razor knife, leaving only the bottom portion of the box suited for carrying groceries. The man bought us every kind of food we were accustomed to eating. What can't be explained is how he knew the brands my mother always bought when she shopped!

The groceries he bought us were: 5 lbs. of flour, 5 lbs. of corn-meal, 1 lb. of coffee, 3 lbs. shortening, 5 lbs. potatoes, 1 can baking powder, pinto beans, salt, a cut of meat, 1 dozen eggs, and 2 cans of Pet brand milk.

The stranger paid for everything; then he and Dad left the market together, heading for the car. Once at the car, the man climbed into the passenger side while my puzzled father loaded the groceries into the back seat. The stranger directed my father to a gas station and, on the way, he handed Dad a ten-dollar bill to pay for the gas he would need to make it home. Confused, my father insisted the man leave him his address so that arrangements could be made to repay the debt. The stranger produced a soft smile and simply said, "It's all been taken care of."

At the station, Dad got out of the car as was his custom and talked to the kid pumping gas. One minute later, Dad turned, and the stranger was nowhere to be seen.

"Now where did he go?" Dad asked the attendant, his eyes actively searching all the while.

"Where did who go?" the kid asked cautiously.

"Oh, that black fella in the car with me."

"What black fella?" the kid replied.

"He was just here a minute ago . . ." Dad started noticing the look of mounting concern in the youngster's face.

"You're the only one I've seen here today," the kid said as he placed the nozzle back into its holder.

Still, Dad was determined to find the stranger. The kid gazed in amazement as Dad raced through the station, looking everywhere for the black man, who had suddenly vanished from sight. He went into the restrooms and even walked clear around the station, hoping to find the mysterious stranger; but he never saw the man again.

Today, I am forty and can vaguely recall my father's departure, but should I live to be one hundred years old, I shall never forget his return home from San Luis Obispo that day in 1958. Nor will I ever forget the amazing story of how God worked a miracle and saved us all from starvation.

The angels Bitsy R., of San Antonio, Texas, saw were even darker. One summer weekend, she and her husband Rollins had taken some friends down to the coast for some rest, fishing, and fellowship. Bitsy drove over to the Laundromat to do a load of sandy sheets and beach towels. Rollins had taken the car that morning, so Bitsy used her friend's station wagon to take the laundry.

Bitsy wasn't accustomed to driving such a long car, and she somehow backed into a deep culvert as she tried to park.

Upon seeing what she had done, and not knowing to whom to turn for help, she said in an audible and somewhat pleading voice, "Lord, help me!" She was hoping that someone with just the right equipment would come along and pull her out of the ditch.

As she glanced at the highway, she focused on a white car approaching rapidly from the north. It turned in and stopped right in front of the station wagon. Two of the biggest, blackest men Bitsy had ever seen jumped out of the car, opened the trunk, got out a tow chain, and without saying a word attached it to the back of their car and to the front of the station wagon. Within a minute, they had the car out of the ditch.

Dumbfounded and speechless, Bitsy tried to tip them for their efforts, but they politely refused, jumped back into their car, and turned off onto the highway going back north, the direction from whence they had come.

Why would they have come and gone so quickly and deliberately? It seemed as if they had driven to where she was with a single purpose in mind. Something within Bitsy leapt with glee as she began to sense that those two big, beautiful black men were special messengers sent from God to help her in her time of need.

In the spring of 1982, Kenneth N. was invited to speak to a morning prayer group near Springfield, Illinois. Before he spoke, a neighboring pastor shared a remarkable story of his recent trip to Mexico.

He, along with several others, had gone there on a preaching mission. While they were returning, their van developed mechanical problems. After jacking up the van, the pastor crawled under to check out the problem. The jack collapsed, and the weight of the van came down on his chest. His companions quickly grabbed the bumper to lift the van. They weren't able to budge it.

The pastor gasped: "Jesus! Jesus!"

Within a few seconds, a youthful-looking Mexican came running toward them. He was thin and small in stature. He had a smile on his face. As he reached the van, he grabbed the bumper and lifted it. The others also joined him and said that it went up like a feather. As he was freed, the pastor said that he felt his chest expand and the broken bones mend. The visitor then lowered the van, waved to them, and ran in the direction from which he came, until he disappeared on the horizon.

Terri Kelly was excited. The Glendale Pathfinder Club was planning a fifteen-mile hike in Grand Canyon. Eleven-year-old Terri got permission from her father to go ahead and get started on the hike with several other girls. They waved goodbye and eagerly started down the trail.

As the afternoon wore on, excitement gave way to fatigue. The girls sat down to rest under some large rocks.

After a few minutes, the other girls went on, leaving Terri to nurse a blister and wait for her parents. After waiting for twenty minutes, she slowly stood up and started walking again, thinking her parents would soon catch up.

She wandered alone for at least an hour, wondering why she didn't see any other Pathfinders. Then she realized she was not on a path. "Where is the trail?" she muttered to herself as fear began to well up inside.

The hot Arizona sun beat down on her as she sat on a dusty rock and cried. *Why, oh why, didn't I stay with the group? How will I ever find my way to Twin Falls by myself?* She looked up the mile-high canyon walls with a feeling of desperation and hopelessness.

If I sit here long enough, someone is bound to walk by soon, she thought. But later, as the sun started to sink behind the tall red-rock canyon wall, she abandoned the thought of being found.

Despondent, and with tears streaming down her cheeks, Terri cried out to God, "Please, Lord, help me out of this predicament. Guide me back to the trail."

She opened her eyes slowly and blinked in blurry surprise as an elderly Indian moved leisurely toward her. He looked weary as he got closer, and Terri noticed he was leading a shaggy brown donkey.

Terri stood up quickly and asked, "Can you tell me how to get to Havasupai?" The Indian gave her a confused look.

"Twin Falls?" she tried again. Still no answer. Just as discouragement began to overtake her, the Indian motioned for her to follow him. Without hesitation, she trailed behind.

Terri followed the Indian for what seemed hours and started to doubt that they were traveling in the right direction. Then, without warning, the Indian picked up his pace, and Terri found herself running to keep up.

The Indian and donkey scurried out of view as they reached a bend in the canyon. In the seconds it took for Terri to reach the bend, she could not even see a sign that the Indian or donkey had been there. She glanced around her. The Indian and donkey had both vanished!

Wondering what to do next, Terri noticed a well-marked trail with a wooden sign that read TWIN FALLS 2 MILES. She cried for joy, realizing God had sent an angel to guide her back to the trail.

Once again on the right path, Terri reached the campsite around sundown. Running to her mother and father, she embraced them and described the miracle of her colorful native guide. That evening, Terri knelt down and thanked God for her deliverance.

A few years later, Terri moved to Arizona and told the story to her pastor, Dick Duerksen, who published it in 1986 in the *Pacific Union Recorder* (15 December 1986). And that's how it came to be here.

Angela H. writes from Bessemer, Alabama, that her angel wore a blue dress.

I firmly believe that I had an encounter with an angel just before Christmas in 1980. My two nieces were spending a few days with us during the school holidays. I had allowed them to stay up late since they were so excited and had not seen each other in almost a year. I reminded them to be sure to turn off all the electrical items, except my daughter's aquarium, before they went to bed. However, they fell asleep without doing this.

I was awakened about 2:30 a.m. by a woman wearing a blue dress with brown trim. She was shaking my shoulder and saying, "Angela, wake up! Go see the girls *now!*" I looked at her for just a second; then she repeated the message and disappeared.

I jumped up and ran into my daughter's bedroom. The girls were sound asleep. They had left on not only the aquarium light, heater, and pump plugged in on a three-way plug-in, but they had her portable TV, hot curlers, and curling iron all plugged into the extension cord, and all were turned on.

The cord was glowing so hot the insulation was melting. Sparks were shooting from the wall plug. When I grabbed the cord, it burned my hand, so I grabbed a piece of clothing to wrap around it so I could pull it from the wall.

Needless to say, I was shaken! We lived in an old wooden house just outside of the city limits. If I had not been awakened, we all might have died, as I'm sure it would have progressed into a roaring fire within another few minutes.

I woke up my husband and told him what had happened. In our ignorance at the time, we even thought it might have been a ghost, not really knowing about angels. Nevertheless, we thanked God and gave the girls a stern warning to never again let that happen.

Now I firmly believe God sent His angels to warn us, and it saved our lives.

Considering the circumstances, perhaps it would have been inappropriate for an angel disguised as a man to appear at Angela Hatchett's bedside in the middle of the night. But why did the roadside angel who saved Edith R's grandfather appear as a female?

Well, why not?

Anslem Prewitt was born in 1845 and lived to be ninety-two. He began selling Christian books in his late sixties because he was so anxious to spread the news of Jesus' great love and His second coming.

IN THE PRESENCE OF ANGELS

In 1915, when he was seventy, Mr. Prewitt stayed at his grandchildren's home while he was in Cooper, Texas, to deliver some books he had sold earlier in the summer.

Granddaughter Edith remembers how her father loaned her grandfather a buggy and two frisky young mules, whose personalities were vividly depicted by their names, Rat and Jude.

Edith, age seven, and her sister Josephine, five, were jumping up and down with glee over the prospect of getting to spend a whole day riding in the country to "help" Grandfather deliver a heavy load of books. Edith remembers:

It had been a long day for Grandfather, and we were almost home. But as for Josephine and me, we were having a wonderful time listening to his stories and songs.

Then came the accident. Cars were few and far between in those days. But a car came down the road, veering side to side, and headed straight for us. Grandfather got as far as he could into the shallow ditch, but the drunken driver ran into us. The mules lunged forward, throwing Grandfather out of the buggy and onto the doubletree, where he became entangled in the harness and could not move without breaking his arms. I thought, *Oh no! My granddaddy is dead!*

The drunken driver lost no time in getting out of there. Then I heard Josephine crying. She had been thrown out and was between the wheels of the buggy. I was able to pull her back into her seat. But what could I do for Grandfather?

Suddenly, a very tall and extremely strong woman lifted Grandfather up and into the buggy and placed the reins into his hands. She walked swiftly ahead of us for about fifty yards, and we noticed that she wore a long, plain dress. Grandfather tried to hurry the mules ahead so he could thank her, but suddenly she disappeared, and we saw her no more.

The family was not surprised to learn that we were not seriously hurt, because they believed we had been miraculously rescued by an angel. How grateful we were for this wonderful encounter!

Being stranded in a strange city can be a disconcerting experience, as Rose M. knows.

There was a large convention going on in Chicago in August 1944, when Rose and her husband Mac and their two-year-old son arrived there by train from the West Coast en route to Rochester, New York. The train was about four-and-one-half hours late, so they missed their train connection to Rochester. At about 2:30 in the morning, they hailed a cab to take them to a hotel, which, because of the convention, was filled to capacity. They soon learned that all the hotels were full. At the suggestion of their driver, they decided to go to a fourth-rate hotel in a rough part of the city.

As soon as possible the next morning, they were up and out of that hotel. The next train to their destination would be in the early evening, so they spent the day in Grant Park, luggage and all. Rose put the baby to sleep on a blanket, and when the baby wasn't sleeping, she attached a rope to a harness on him and tied the rope to a nearby tree.

When Mac left to try to buy some milk for the baby, a disreputable-looking man came near, giving them searching looks as Rose sat on the blanket beside her sleeping baby. When he saw Mac returning, he beat a hasty retreat.

The day dragged on. Office workers left for home; then those who had been relaxing in Grant Park began to leave. Dusk was gathering, and the family had had little or nothing to eat that day. They sat together in the park on a low concrete ledge surrounding a statue, trying to figure out how to carry their suitcases and baby down the street a few blocks to a corner restaurant.

Finally, a tall, well-dressed, middle-aged woman stopped to talk with them. She volunteered to stay by their luggage so they could go get something to eat. Because she was a woman and appeared to be a trustworthy person, they went to eat and returned quickly so as to not keep her from getting home.

To their surprise, she was in no hurry to leave. She said they should take the early-evening train as they had first planned, even though it made more stops, rather than a later train Mac had decided to take. They would get home sooner and be safer than if they waited in the park for the later train.

The train depot was next to the park, and the train would soon be coming in. The woman graciously insisted on helping carry the luggage. She accompanied them to the depot and stayed with them until they had been assured of space on the train. Before leaving she remarked that they had a beautiful little boy, that they should watch him carefully and let him always know he must obey. Finally, they bid each other goodbye, with the couple expressing their gratitude. By then it was quite dark.

Was it an angel? Was some unknown peril thus averted? Someday we'll know.

The Bible makes it clear that God has a soft spot in His heart for widows. "A father to the fatherless, a defender of widows, is God in his holy dwelling" (Psalm 68:5); "the Lord watches over the alien and sustains the fatherless and the widow" (Psalm 146:9). He hears their unspoken cry, even before they pray.

Barbara D., of Lavalette, West Virginia, remembers how, when she was just a little girl, a mysterious woman touched her life.

My father died at an early age after a serious illness and left behind my mother and four daughters, ages nine, eleven, thirteen, and seventeen. Dad had done all the managing of the household, and my mother was ill-equipped to take over in his absence.

Since we had no car, we walked a lot or relied on kind neighbors. This one particular Saturday, we were going to town to get glasses for my sister Wilma. We walked about a mile to the bus stop and went into town. A parade had disrupted traffic, so it took a long time to get to the office and pick up the glasses. Then we discovered that the street where we would usually catch our bus home was closed to traffic.

Before we could think of what to do, a nice woman walked up to us. She was very pale in complexion and had long, flowing blond hair. Although it was early in May, she carried a white-as-snow sweater over her arm.

As she talked, she was sliding her foot in and out of her shoe. My mother looked down and asked if her shoes were hurting her feet. She said, "Oh no, I'm just not used to wearing shoes."

And then she said, "Your bus is waiting for you just around that corner." We had not talked about waiting for a bus or wondering where to find it. As we stared after her, she turned and walked off, disappearing around the corner of a building.

As we walked in the direction she had given us, we looked for her but couldn't find her anywhere. But, just as she had instructed, the city bus was waiting for us where she had said it would be.

The bus driver was sitting patiently. When we started up the steps, he exclaimed, "Well, you're finally here! I've been waiting for you!" He had not been the driver we came in with that morning. As we asked how he knew we were coming, he just smiled.

My family and I believe that this was an encounter with an angel.

IN THE PRESENCE OF ANGELS

Beulah B., of Hot Springs, Arkansas, and her husband were married during the Great Depression. They had no home of their own, so they moved frequently. They had just moved to a new neighborhood where they didn't know anyone.

Beulah and a woman minister teamed up to hold a revival. Beulah led the singing and music; her friend preached. One night a new woman came in. No one knew her. She gave a wonderful testimony, and Beulah noticed she had a small suitcase with her.

When the service was over, no one offered to take the woman for the night, so Beulah asked her minister friend if she would take her home, since she had an extra bedroom. She flatly refused.

I just couldn't leave that woman alone there, so I told her she was welcome to go home with me. I knew I didn't have food, and I would have to put up a cot for her to sleep on. She seemed happy and thanked me. Before retiring, she offered the sweetest prayer. The next morning, I went out to walk and talk with God, for I didn't know what I would do about breakfast. As I went by the chicken house, I looked inside, not expecting to find an egg, for the few hens I had were in a strange place and wouldn't lay.

To my surprise, there in a makeshift nest were two pretty, fresh eggs.

I hurried inside to fix them for our guest. She came into the kitchen and said, "Sister, if it's OK with you, I'll take the ends of the bread; I like them." So the breakfast problem was solved; I had only ends.

After she ate, she prayed again for us, that God would supply all our needs. Then she said she must go and stepped outside. At that moment, I remembered I hadn't told her that the bus station was only two blocks down the street. I opened the door to tell her, but she was nowhere in sight.

Since I lived on a corner, I was able to see down four streets. I looked in all directions, but she was out of sight. I believed she was an angel, and no one can make me doubt.

CHAPTER

15

Strangers in the Night

Around the turn of the century, a little-known Austrian doctor by the name of Lorenz developed a new surgical technique to cure a disease formerly considered incurable. He became famous, and so Dr. Lorenz was asked to do a lecture tour of the United States, working from coast to coast and meeting as many American physicians and surgeons as possible. During this time there was opportunity for very few actual operations—and this makes what happened in a midwestern city especially poignant.

IN THE PRESENCE OF ANGELS

Toward the close of a busy day, Dr. Lorenz managed to slip past the attendants posted to take care of him. He made his way out into the street for some fresh air and exercise. Soon it began to rain. He decided to ask for help at the nearest house.

An urgent couple of rings led to the door's being opened just wide enough to reveal two sad eyes topped by some tousled graying hair. The middle-aged woman listened as the request was made in hesitant English: "The rain . . . May I . . . ? Shelter . . . ?"

She almost agreed. But then she murmured: "There's trouble enough in this house already. Go somewhere else." After that, the door closed, and the would-be guest turned back to the street again—only to see a taxi hired by his hosts pull to the curb. Within minutes, he was preparing for his evening meal.

But what of the sad-faced woman? She returned to the bedroom where her daughter was lying in bed—the victim of what had been called an incurable disease.

She had heard that the one man in the world who was able to treat the disease was visiting in her city that week. She had prayed for help, and what had God sent her? Just a barely coherent, dripping old man, standing on her doorstep.

The following day, she saw Dr. Lorenz's photograph in the paper. She realized what she had done and wrote a letter to the newspaper. "I did not know . . ." she said.[1]

It pays to befriend strangers—even when they're not angels.

Tom H. and his family were on their way to buy groceries in town. About five miles from town, Mr. H. noticed an elderly gentleman walking along the highway in the opposite direction. There was something about the man that attracted attention; perhaps his smile. He was visibly tired. He was dressed in old clothing, but he appeared neat and clean.

On the way back, the man was still walking, so Tom invited him to ride home with them. His shoes had holes in them, and his feet were dusty and blistered, so when they got home, Tom's wife took a basin and towel and washed his feet. He was very friendly and affable, very kindly in appearance, and the children took to him right away. He took them on his lap and told them stories. He was very positive and seemed to have a close, personal friendship with God. He ate dinner and spent the night.

In the morning the man shared some more encouraging words from the Bible. He said little about himself, except that he was going another hundred miles or so down the highway to visit someone. The family gave him some money for bus fare.

But before he left, he shared an experience he had had in town. He didn't seem to be complaining, just giving some needful information. He had stopped at a certain man's house and asked for water, and the man had told him that he wasn't in the habit of helping strangers and that he should be on his way.

This was important information for Tom's folks, because they were thinking about investing with this man. But based on the new information, they decided not to do that.

Soon it became clear that they had made a wise decision, because this man turned out to be not all that he pretended to be, and he left town shortly after that.

Maybe this wasn't a man from heaven. We don't know. But we feel that he was an angel to us, a messenger from God, and he gave us hope and guidance and encouragement. We've always been grateful that we were not forgetful to entertain strangers.

Angels have rescued people from automobile accidents, from

rape, from drowning, from being lost in the woods. But sometimes angels come, not to do what we want, but to see if we'll do what God wants. Sometimes angels are God's exam agents sent to test us, just as they tested the people of Sodom.

Sodom was the city God destroyed by fire. Here's the story. Thousands of years ago, God sent some angels disguised as weary travelers to Abraham. The story is found in chapters 18 and 19 of the book of Genesis. Notice how Abraham treated these travelers. He begged them to stop and rest and said: "Let a little water be brought, and then you may all wash your feet and rest under this tree. Let me get you something to eat, so you can be refreshed and then go on your way" (Genesis 18:4, 5).

Then he killed his choicest calf and threw a feast for the men. In return for his selfless hospitality, Abraham was given a son! Before they left, these men (who were really angels) told Abraham that Sarah would miraculously conceive in her old age and bear him a long-promised heir.

Then the Lord told Abraham that Sodom had such a bad reputation that He was going to drop by to see how bad the situation really was. So He sent the angels on to Sodom, where they met with a very different response. The local citizens offered no hospitality; they simply wanted to use these strangers for their own perverted pleasure. So God destroyed Sodom by fire. Ezekiel 6:49 sums up the situation this way: "Now this was the sin of your sister Sodom: She and her daughters were arrogant, overfed and unconcerned; *they did not help the poor and needy.*"

Poor and needy seems to be one of God's favorite disguises. Matthew 24 says that God separates the righteous from the wicked according to the way they have treated the unfortunate. "If you visit the sick," God says, "you visit Me. The clothes you give to the needy, you give to Me." That's exciting! By befriending the down and out, we are befriending God. He hides behind trembling lips and pleading eyes. Behind each tear-stained face, each reaching hand, one way or another, is God. "I was a stranger," He says, "and you invited me in" (Matthew 24:35).

In fact, God's greatest entrance into history was in disguise. The Jews in the days of Jesus were expecting a Messiah who was a mighty king, a military conqueror to deliver them from the Romans. So what did God send them? A humble peasant carpenter. "He had no beauty or majesty to attract us to him, nothing in his appearance that we should desire him." So "he was despised and rejected by men" (Isaiah 53:2, 3).

At Sinai He came in strength, as an awesome deity. At Bethlehem He came in weakness, as a helpless child. Who would have thought?

God still comes to us in disguise. Sometimes He comes to us with pain, like Jacob's midnight wrestler. He whose garment is light sometimes wraps himself in robes of thickest darkness. "The Lord has said that he would dwell in a dark cloud" (1 Kings 8:12); "he made darkness his covering, his canopy around him" (Psalm 18:11). Sometimes we have to be tested in the darkness before we are ready for the light.

So God likes to play little tricks, like sending His angels in the guise of a tramp, to see if we are people of compassion. That's why Hebrews 13:2 says, "Do not forget to entertain strangers, for by so doing some people have entertained angels without knowing it."

Miriam S. recalls a time when her father said No to an angel. It was a special night when several Christian families of the community were coming to her home in Finland for a Bible study. Each Friday found them in a different home, but today they would come to Miriam's home, and some would spend the night. Miriam's family were happy to entertain guests.

The study for this evening was based on Matthew 22:39, which says "love thy neighbor."

IN THE PRESENCE OF ANGELS

"To me that means I'll lend a helping hand whenever I see the opportunity to do so," said one neighbor.

"We as Christians surely cannot pass along unpleasant stories about others, or even listen to them, if we obey that commandment," offered another.

The study continued until at last it was time to close with prayer. As the last Amen was said, Miriam's family heard a noise in the kitchen. There, just inside the door, stood a ragged old man with a paper in his hand. Father took the paper and read, "I'm deaf and mute. I need a place to sleep tonight. Can you help me?"

As the family discussed the matter, they realized that all their beds were filled. "Oh, I know," said Mother; "he can go to the guest home next door. I know they have room over there."

Miriam's father wrote a message on the back of the paper, directing the man next door. After reading the note, the old man turned, walked out the back door, and was gone.

When Father came back to the study table, he was serious and quiet. Suddenly, he exclaimed, "We have just had an opportunity to put into practice what we have learned tonight, and we have not accepted it. I must call that man back, and we will *make* room for him."

Quickly going to the back door, he tried to turn the doorknob, but the door was locked. "Didn't that fellow just now go out this door?" he said to himself. Unlocking it, he hurried to the outside door. It, too, was still locked, as he had left it an hour earlier.

As he looked out across the yard, there was not a footprint to be seen in the freshly fallen snow. Rushing out into the lighted street, Father looked up and down. Not a soul in sight! The visitor had disappeared.

"I am sure," said Miriam's father, "that an angel visited our home last night, but we had no room for him. Oh, if only God would test me again!"

During the next ten years, this was the burden of Miriam's father's prayers: "O Lord, test me once more!"

Well, they did have another chance. The family moved into a

smaller house, with very little room, even for themselves. One evening as they were sitting down to their evening meal, a knock sounded at the door. When the door was opened, there stood a beggar. His clothes were patched and so dirty that Miriam could smell them across the room. On his arms were running boils.

"Please, sir, I'm hungry and so cold, and as yet I have found no place to sleep tonight."

"Come in, come in!" said Father, almost pulling the man into the room, thinking, *"God is giving me another chance, and I must not fail Him this time."*

That night after a good meal and a warm bath, the beggar slept in Miriam's father's bed while her father tried to rest on the floor beside him. Often during the night he got up to change the dressing on the boils. The next day, as Father took the man to the hospital for treatment, he said, "Never again will I fail to love my neighbor as myself, as it says in Matthew 22:39."

Mrs. Ruth W., of Apopka, Florida, was living in Carol City, Florida. She had a habit of praying at twelve o'clock noon every day. On one particular day, she had just gotten off her knees, when the doorbell rang. When she opened the door, she found herself talking through the locked screen door to a young man about nineteen years old who asked her to unlock the door. When she asked why, he said he was hungry. He had been walking all morning, trying to sell religious books to pay his way through Oakwood College.

I told him I couldn't buy any books, but I could feed him. I told him I didn't eat meat—all I had were breakfast patties and vegetables. He said that was fine, since they didn't eat meat at Oakwood. He ate two plates full. He kept watching me, and we talked about how hard it was to get people to buy the books. I told him that mainly old, retired people lived in this section. He said, "Thank you kindly. You are so kind."

I told him, "I try to be kind to everyone." The stranger then left.

My son was in his room looking out and said to me, "Mother, who were you talking to? I got up and came down the hallway, and you were sitting at the table talking to yourself."

I asked him, "Didn't you see the young man at the table eating?"

He answered, "There was no one at the table but you."

I told him to go to the door and look down the street. My son and I went to the corner and never saw anyone. I couldn't figure it out until I prayed before I went to bed and saw that same man's face in the form of an angel standing in my room.

When Jesus walked this earth, He always seemed to associate with the helpless and the powerless. So if you want to find Jesus, if you want angels to visit you, then you'd better get busy loving the outcasts and the problem people who cross your path in life, for that's the most likely way to encounter Jesus Christ.

Here is another story of a mysterious visitor, as told by Marion F. Ash, in *Insight*, May 30, 1992.

Mother's favorite Bible verse was: "Do not forget to entertain strangers, for by so doing some people have entertained angels without knowing it" (Hebrews 13:2). And Mother seldom passed up an opportunity to act on this text.

Just once did she almost weaken. I remember the time well because my baby sister was very sick. Father had phoned the doctor in our neighboring village, but the man was sick and couldn't come. The roads were covered with deep snow, and Father said it was risky trying to take her to the city hospital.

All morning Mother had placed cold cloths on Lucy's forehead, hoping to run the fever down. I had been standing at the window watching the snowflakes as they sailed down from the clouds. And that's when I saw an old man struggling up the lane that led to the house.

"Someone's coming!" I exclaimed.

Father came to the window and looked. "It's an old tramp," he said simply. In those days of the Depression, tramps were a common sight, on good days as well as bad.

Mother, who seldom turned a tramp away without giving him something to eat, said to Father, "Better tell him to go on. Tell him we have sickness in the family."

Father looked at Mother with sort of a shocked expression. He had never taken much stock in Hebrews 13:2. More than once he had told Mother that if she didn't stop feeding all the old tramps that passed our way, we'd find ourselves in the poorhouse. I sometimes agreed with Father because on several occasions, after Mother had fed two or three unfortunate ones, we had barely enough food left in the house for ourselves.

Father spoke to Mother, and I could see a satisfied expression on his face. "Well, it's about time you came to your senses. There has to be a line drawn someplace, and it might as well be now."

When the old man knocked, Father went to the door, and I could tell by the look on his face that he was all prepared to tell the old tramp to move on.

Mother and I followed Father across the room, and when the door was opened, we saw the face of a very old man. His thick stocking cap was pulled low over his ears, and his long beard was covered with snowflakes. His topcoat was thin and ragged, and he wore no gloves. In one hand his fingers clutched a little bag, and I knew it contained his entire stock of worldly possessions.

"Could you spare an old man a cup of tea and a bit to eat?" he asked in a weak, pleading voice. "I stopped at the house up the road, but no one answered the door. I guess no one was at home."

Before Father had time to turn the old man away, Mother said, "Let him in, Frank. He's welcome to stay for lunch."

I saw a frown on Father's face, and I knew he was displeased. But he moved aside so the old man could enter.

A smile came to the old man's face, and his eyes looked less tired and sad. "God bless you," he said in a trembling voice.

Father helped him remove his topcoat and told him to take a chair beside the big heating stove. On the way to the chair, the old man passed the crib where Baby Lucy lay sleeping.

"She's awful sick," Mother explained. "We tried to get our family doctor, but he's taken ill."

For a long while, the old man stood by the crib and looked at Lucy. "She reminds me of a little daughter I once had." He put one of his hands on hers. "She has a burning fever, doesn't she?"

For another moment, he stood, letting his hand rest ever so lightly on hers. Then, turning to Mother, he said, "Looks like a little angel, doesn't she?"

Mother nodded, and I could tell she had suddenly become all choked up. "I'll get some lunch," she mumbled and hurried into the kitchen.

The old man sat down in the chair and extended his hands toward the stove, rubbing them together to get the blood circulating once more. Father went to the stove and threw another chunk of wood in, then pushed it in place with the iron poker. "Where are you heading?" he finally asked.

Father asked this question of all the tramps Mother fed. "Not that it does any good," he once remarked. "Most of them don't know where they're going, and they wouldn't tell you if they did."

But just the same, I was curious, so I stepped closer to the stove to hear the answer.

"Alabama," the old man answered.

Father nearly dropped the hot poker on the rug. "Alabama? That's hundreds of miles from here!"

The old man nodded agreement. "My son lives there."

I would have liked to listen to more of the conversation, but Mother was calling me from the kitchen. "Would you please set the table?" she said when I went to see what she wanted.

As I began working at my task, I kept thinking about the old man. Once, I looked at Mother as she worked over the stove, and I wondered if she was thinking about her favorite Bible verse. More than likely, Hebrews 13:2 had been pushed aside by her concern over Baby Lucy, for twice while we worked, she carried cold cloths into the living room to put on Lucy's forehead.

I had just finished setting the table when Father came into the kitchen. "The old man's taking a nap," he said. "He seems like he's entirely worn out. Why don't these old bums try to go to the shelters the churches are providing for them during this cold weather? He's crazy. Says he's aiming to go to Alabama to see his son. If you ask me, he'll never make it. Not in this kind of weather."

Mother didn't say a word; she just handed Father a canning jar of beets to open.

"Why, this is the jar of beets that won you a blue ribbon at the county fair," Father exclaimed. "I thought you were saving it for a special occasion."

"This is a special occasion," Mother answered, and I would have loved to know how she figured it unless it was that Hebrews 13:2 verse again.

I noticed that same frown on Father's face. "OK, OK," he said as he twisted the lid off. "I just hope that someday you'll get paid for all your troubles."

"Oh, I will," Mother exclaimed, and I never heard her speak so positively about anything.

Before calling the old man to lunch, Mother placed another cold cloth on Lucy's forehead. "If she's not better by morning, we'll have to get her to a doctor somehow," she said, and Father agreed.

239

IN THE PRESENCE OF ANGELS

I don't remember what all Mother prepared for lunch that cold winter day, but knowing Mother, it was sufficient. It must have looked very appealing to the old man as he sat down, for I could see something in his eyes that I couldn't quite fathom. All I remember is that he looked at Mother and in a very low voice asked if she'd mind if he said grace. Mother looked both shocked and pleased, and when she nodded her approval, we all bowed our heads.

"Dear precious Lord," the old man began, his voice so low I could hardly hear him, "it is with a thankful but humble heart I come to Thee. Thou, in Thy great mercy, hast led me to this home where love abounds. Where from their hearts, these good people have willingly set a bounteous feast before me. May Your blessings always rest upon them." He paused for a moment and then said, "And precious Lord, lay Your healing hand upon their baby girl. Amen."

When I looked up, I saw tears in Mother's eyes, and Father's hands trembled as he passed the platter of potatoes across the table to the old man. At that moment, I wondered what Father's idea was now about the unworthiness of old tramps. I would have loved to know if he had any thoughts about entertaining angels.

I don't remember if all the food was eaten, but I do know that the old man kept eating red beets until they were all gone. "I never tasted such good beets," he exclaimed. "When Kate—that was my wife—was living, she'd can all of them she could get her hands on."

Shortly after finishing lunch, the old man declared that he'd better be leaving. He said that he wanted to make it as far as the next village before sundown. Mother left the table and went into the back bedroom. When she came out, she was carrying one of Father's discarded topcoats and a pair of gloves.

"We'd like for you to have these," she said, handing them to the old man.

With trembling hands, he took the offered gifts. "Thanks. You people have been so kind to me. The Lord will surely bless you for it."

In the front room, the old man paused by Lucy's crib. He looked at the sleeping child for a moment and then laid his hand on her forehead. I was sure I saw his lips moving. No one said a word, but we all noticed.

Then he put on his wraps and started for the door. On the front porch, the old man turned and looked at us. We saw tears in his eyes, and his voice trembled when he spoke. "Goodbye, dear friends. I'll not be passing this way again. May God's richest blessings rest upon you."

We watched as he waded through the deep snow back to the main road. We watched until the swirling snow obscured him from our sight.

Mother was the first to go back into the house. "Lucy!" we heard her cry.

Father and I dashed inside just in time to see Mother lifting my baby sister from her crib. Mother looked happier than I had ever seen her.

She turned to us. "She was sitting up when I came in," she exclaimed. "And just feel her—her fever is gone."

Father just stood there smiling. He offered no explanation for the sudden turn of events, and neither did Mother. But I knew what they were thinking. It was Hebrews 13:2 again.

One thing I'm sure about—two miracles happened. Baby Lucy's fever was gone, and Father had a complete change of heart. Had we, on that cold winter day, entertained an angel?

It was a stormy night at a small hotel in Philadelphia. An elderly man and woman approached the registration desk and asked for a room, explaining that all of the big hotels seemed to be full. The clerk explained that there were several conventions in town and indeed, there were no rooms to be had anywhere that night. He also pointed out that all of their rooms were full as well—but added, "I wouldn't feel right about turning you out on such a night; would you be willing to sleep in my room?"

The couple were a bit taken aback at his offer, but the young man insisted that it would work out fine. The next day, as the elderly couple was checking out, the man told the clerk, "You are the kind of man who should be the boss of the best hotel in the country. Maybe someday I'll build one for you." They all smiled at the little joke, and then the clerk helped them carry their bags out to the street.

Two years later, the clerk received a letter from the old man. He had almost forgotten the incident, but the letter recalled that night and included a round-trip ticket to New York, asking the young man to pay them a visit.

When the young fellow reached New York, the old man led him to the corner of Fifth Avenue and Thirty-Fourth Street and pointed to a great new building there, a palace of reddish stone with turrets and watchtowers like a castle from fairyland. The older man said, "That is the hotel I have just built for you to manage."

"You must be joking!"

"I am certainly not joking." The old man just stood there and smiled.

The young man asked, "Who—who are you? That you can do this?"

"My name is William Waldorf Astor."

That hotel was the original Waldorf-Astoria, and the young clerk who became the first manager was George C. Boldt.

Be kind to strangers. It's not a bad idea.

---

1. Trevor Lloyd, "You Did Not Know!" *Adventist Professional—Special Feature: Turning the Church Upside Down*, 4:1, 29.

CHAPTER

16

You Can Be an Angel

Ever wondered what it's like to be an angel? Well, there's no need to wonder. Why not try it?

True, certain tasks require the split-second intervention of an honest-to-goodness seraph. But usually, when God needs an agent, angels are His second choice.

Human beings are His first. Kris Coffin often wondered about angels and wished one would put on a disguise and come to her aid in a time of need. But was it angels she encountered? You be the judge. . . .

Everyone has heard angel stories. The kind that go,

243

IN THE PRESENCE OF ANGELS

"It was a cold, dark night, and we were lost . . ." Suddenly, someone appears from nowhere and rescues the protagonists. And when they turn around—you guessed it—the rescuer is gone. (Although they could see for miles in any direction.)

I used to imagine the fun the angels must have picking out their disguises.

"You look absolutely ridiculous in those overalls, Gabriel."

"Not a Ford pickup again! The brakes squeak."

"Try the blue one on again. . . . Actually, I think white's really your color."

"Don't disappear until they turn around. And remember to take the truck with you. This isn't the rapture."

Can you see it? There's a big room with a WARDROBE sign over the door. As you enter, an angel with a clipboard asks your destination.

"Wyoming," you say.

"Ah yes," says the angel. "Go up this aisle past the saris, and make a left by the kimonos."

You emerge wearing cowboy boots, a plaid flannel shirt, and jeans. You enter another room labeled PROPS. Inside are rows of cars, trucks, and rickshas. Lifesaving equipment lines the walls.

"Give me an '83 Dodge Ram," you tell the attendant. "And throw a couple of bales of hay in the back."

"Coming right up," he says. "And don't forget to stop by MAKEUP for that suntanned look."

But it doesn't happen that way, right?

I had heard enough of these stories that I was prepared when it happened to me.

It was a hot, bright day when suddenly *thump, thump, thump* at sixty miles per hour in the fast lane. We were on a very long freeway bridge with no shoulders. We pulled into the right lane and stopped. Our tire looked like shredded wheat. Two young women, alone, in the city, with a spare and jack but no wrench.

You Can Be an Angel

Zoom! A semi roared by us, just barely missing our car. We flattened ourselves against the guardrail. Cars screeched to a stop behind us. I was terrified. "OK, God," I said. "Now's the time. Bring on the angels."

A white Camaro pulled up and stopped. Then two big, dangerous-looking men got out. The kind who make you lock your car doors and roll up your windows when you go by them. One was very tall and wore shades, but it was the other man that I noticed. He was wearing what looked like bedroom slippers over athletic socks, and he had a greasy baseball cap over his cornrow-braided hair. On his vest were rows and rows of buttons—the kind that usually say "Smile! Have a happy day!" or "I love Pookie." His didn't say "Have a happy day." I can't tell you what they said. The printing press would break down. I mean, no guardian angel, no matter how adventurous, would wear buttons that said that.

I tried not to stare in innocent horror. We must have shown our nervousness, because he asked us in a puzzled way, "Why are you girls acting so leery of us?" What could I say?

But I still wasn't going to miss my only chance, so I watched carefully as they helped us drive our lame beast slowly off the bridge and change the tire with their wrench. I didn't turn around even once, and I actually took two pictures of them changing the tire. I was rewarded by watching them drive off in their Camaro and make a right at a stop sign.

Back on the freeway (I missed my plane, but maybe it was hijacked anyway), I mused about our "angels." Outfitting Gabriel to come to our rescue might have been more exciting, but it wouldn't have let those two guys experience the "good Samaritan" feeling. Or us realize that there are good people in all parts of society. We were in desperate need, and God provided people to help people.

We were created a little lower than the angels. Giving of ourselves to help others is uplifting. Maybe even that much.

IN THE PRESENCE OF ANGELS

There was one button on the man's vest that I can quote. It said "You're in good company when you're with me."[1]

Helping others is so rewarding that God wants to let sinful human beings in on the fun, as it tends to have a transforming effect on them. Angels have had their chance; they've had thousands of years of practice at it; now it's our turn.

The word *angel* simply means "messenger," and it is used in the Bible of human messengers (see 1 Kings 19:2; Malachi 3:1; Luke 7:24). Haggai is called "the Lord's messenger." His encouraging message was " 'I am with you,' declares the Lord" (Haggai 1:13). Another angel in the flesh was Epaphroditus, whom Paul describes as "my brother, fellow worker and fellow soldier, who is also your messenger, whom you sent to take care of my needs" (Philippians 2:25). Sometimes teachers are God's messengers:

For the lips of a priest ought to preserve knowledge, and
from his mouth men should seek instruction—because he
is the messenger of the Lord Almighty (Malachi 2:7).

The word translated "messenger" in these verses is usually translated "angel." Just as Epaphroditus was an angel to Paul, so you can be to someone else in need.

Isaiah chapter 6 pictures God as sitting on His throne in heaven surrounded by hosts of angels singing His praises. Yet when He wants to send a message to His people, He calls for a messenger who comes from among the people He wishes to reach. Isaiah overheard God saying, "Whom shall I send? And who will go for us?" His immediate answer was, "Here am I. Send me!" (Isaiah 6:8).

So what's your answer?

God is still calling for a few good men and women to represent Him to others by becoming channels of His grace. The only requirements are love (we suspect that angels instinctively love people in the same way that people instinctively love babies) and a spirit that is tuned to the subtle whisper of His voice.

To show how God takes care of His own, I want to tell how an angel sent me to visit an eighty-year-old woman who was ill.

I was working at the nursing home connected with Hylandale Academy in Wisconsin thirty years ago. My son was attending the academy, and my daughter was in church school there.

I usually did the baking and cooking for the place, but for a short time I worked the night shift.

One Friday afternoon when alone in my room, a voice spoke out clearly, "Go visit someone."

I inquired, "Who shall I go to see—the blind woman at the home?"

The voice said, "Go see Mrs. Hallock." She was the widow of the founder of the school.

Two boys were going there to drop off the mailbag for the next day's mail, which the mailman always dropped off at her home. I told them to ask if she was feeling well.

The voice insisted, "You go see her yourself." It repeated this command two more times.

I hurried down the sandy road singing "Now I belong to Jesus, Jesus belongs to me, not for the years of time alone, but for eternity." Large flakes of snow mixed with rain were falling as I hurried along.

When I reached Mrs. Hallock's home, I was going to explain it all to her, but she asked: "You were impressed to come?"

I said, "Yes, I was impressed to come."

She said, "I just placed a nitroglycerine tablet into my mouth under my tongue."

IN THE PRESENCE OF ANGELS

I knew then that she was not in the best of health, and she said she would call her neighbor to come spend the night with her.

I hurried to her home the next morning and found out that she had had a bad night and was glad to have her neighbor with her.

—Esther C., Marvell, Arkansas.

Here is a similar story from the late fifties. William Reichard's class had been studying the account of Philip and the Ethiopian court official in Acts. During the course of the discussion, someone asked, "God no longer sends angels to tell people where to go, does He?"

"Given the need and the circumstances, I believe He could and would, the same now as then," William answered. We continue with the story in William's words:

"God, give me a positive answer," I silently prayed.

The following afternoon, I was visiting with old friends, retired Pastor and Mrs. J. F. Hurlbut, on 10th Street. Along in the afternoon, I was suddenly aware of a quiet voice: "You have to go over to Lewiston this evening. "Where in Lewiston?" my mind inquired, but there was no answer.

"I have to go over to Lewiston this evening, so I'll bid you goodbye," I told my friends.

William knew only one family who lived across the Snake River in Lewiston, Idaho, but when he went by their home, it was dark. A slow drive down Main Street revealed no one in obvious need.

Back on G Street, I got out of my car and stood until the night chill became too much, then started back toward Clarkston.

At 16th, again that voice: "You have to go over to Main Street." So I turned and walked the long, dark block to the lights of Main Street.

On down Main Street, in front of the VFW Building, a darkened car was standing at the curb with the engine running. Quickly stepping closer, I saw a man lying in the front seat asleep. The smoky engine exhaust was blowing back under the old relic.

Carbon monoxide! I stepped to jerk the door open, then

thought, *What if he is sleeping on a gun? This is for the police.*
William went to the rear of a nearby building and called the police.

Before I could walk fifty feet to the front of the building, a police car went past at fifty miles an hour, with red lights flashing. A policeman jumped out and ran to the old car. With one fluid motion, he threw the door open with his left hand and jerked the man out by the collar with his right.

As I reached the street again, the two officers were getting the unconscious man into their car.

The car backed out with siren sounding, and I watched it race a mile up the hill to the hospital in less than a minute.

The other officer walked back to the old car, turned off the ignition, and locked the doors. He was backing out to the street when I stepped up.

"What is it?" he asked.

"I'm the man who called in."

"You probably just saved a man's life." Probably? God doesn't work in probabilities.[2]

Sometimes God uses people as His messengers, even before they come to know Him. F. S., of Moreno Valley, California, recalls such a time in his own life:

One day ten years ago, before I knew the Lord, I was camped at Lake Mead in Nevada. The day was very windy, with gusts up to one hundred mph, as a tropical storm had just passed over the area. I had a twenty-three-foot boat in the water in a cove that kept it protected from the wind.

Often when these storms pass over this lake, which is one hundred miles long, many boats sink. It was late in the afternoon when I got the idea that I wanted to go for a boat ride. The sea was heavy with six-foot whitecaps. My wife said, "You're crazy! Don't take the dog with you." It was an urge I had to satisfy.

As I got about five miles out into the lake, I saw a smaller boat dead in the water. I couldn't see anyone on board. As I swung around its stern, at a distance, I could see a man praying in the bow of the boat.

I came alongside his boat and threw him a rope and towed him into the marina.

Well, I didn't know our Lord then or the power of prayer, but as I look back today, I thank the Lord for letting me be His vessel, even though I didn't understand at the time what compelled me to go for a boat ride that day.

Mrs. Lela K., of Hanford, California, tells about her experience of feeding a stranger who knocked at her door for directions and said she was hungry. Afterward the woman said, "God bless you," and kissed Lela's hand. Lela never saw her again. But on another occasion, Lela was the one needing help.

I took the morning bus to town to get a perm. When I was ready to go home, I went over to Imperial Savings to ask someone to call the bus for me. I asked them how long it would be before the bus would arrive. They said twenty or thirty minutes. I decided to wait outside on a bench.

After an hour, the bus still hadn't arrived, and my back was starting to hurt. I was about to go back into the bank, when a woman came down the street. I commented to her, "That bus is something else. I've waited for an hour, and it hasn't shown up. My back is hurting too."

You Can Be an Angel

The stranger asked me where I lived and offered to take me home. On the way home, she said she came from the San Diego area and had been living here for about a year and a half, adding that she tries to do at least one good deed a day. I told her I sure hope God blesses her. She answered, "How do you know your guardian angel didn't send me to you?"

Whatever the case, I was so thankful for her being there. I'm sure there have been many other times that God's angels have helped me, and I praise them for it.

Angels are so strong they can stop armies. They are breathtakingly beautiful and more talented than any living human being. So when you think about it, it does seem ridiculous, doesn't it, for God to assign these glorious beings to the mundane tasks of being auto mechanics, bodyguards, and nursemaids to children. They are overqualified. It's sort of like hiring Queen Elizabeth to clean your house.

But it only seems ridiculous because our priorities on planet Earth are so distorted. In this world the power structures work like this: the beautiful people are served by the less talented and beautiful, and the more underlings one has, the higher the status. But the kingdom of heaven is quite different. There, the law of life is that the beautiful and talented lovingly serve those of lesser means. In heaven, service is status, and one excels by excelling in ministry. It is only by faithful devotion to the needs of those weaker and less fortunate that we advance into ever greater intimacy with God. The happiest people on earth are those who live to make others happy. That's why you should be an angel.

It is not necessary to wait to hear a voice from heaven telling you to go see so-and-so. You don't have to look very far to find a need. It may be nothing more than a neighbor working on his transmission.

IN THE PRESENCE OF ANGELS

Last summer, the transmission in my work truck required repair. This is a two-man job unless you have specialized equipment. I am a shade-tree mechanic with only bare necessities in tools. However, I had endeavored to accomplish the job myself. As I lay under the truck working away with my limited knowledge, a neighbor leaned over, spoke, slid under, and began helping.

The job took all day and some heavy, close cooperation. As I lay on my back next to my neighbor, an enormous wave of appreciation swept over me. There was never any request for pay or reciprocation; just a neighbor helping a neighbor. The inner voice said, "Be careful to entertain strangers. They may be angels unawares."

This fellow was no stranger, but he was sent of God. He was the one "unaware" of why he was helping. He was an angel unaware.

—Donald A., Knoxville, Tennessee.

Here are some more creative ideas for ways you can be an angel. No doubt you will be able to come up with many more. It is only fair to warn you that these ideas are addictive. If you do this sort of thing on a regular basis, you're liable to become so happy you will not know how to live with yourself.

Mark your calendar so you can send a note to someone who has lost a child or a spouse on the first anniversary of his or her death.

Give your spouse a certificate good for a free backrub.

Have pizza delivered to your local fire department.

At a public arena, park, or beach, buy out the vender's entire stock of newspapers, balloons, gum, etc., and pass them out free to people around you.

Offer to help a classmate with homework.

Call up your pastor, and ask if he has anyone who needs a friendly visit.

On a hot day, just before the mail is delivered, write a note and place a cold drink on your mailbox.

Who is the loneliest person you know? Do something to make him or her feel loved.

Write letters to the residents in a local nursing home.

Give your spouse a certificate that entitles him or her to one free day of your time, in which your activities will be totally controlled by your spouse.

Mow your neighbors' lawn while they're away.

Buy soft drinks for everyone on the bus.

Bake cupcakes, and hand them out at work or in class.

Forgive someone for an injustice.

Draw happy faces, and write "God Loves You" on all the blackboards.

Bake a dish/bread/pie for your neighbor or your boss.

Find someone who looks unhappy, and write him or her an anonymous note.

Buy a treat for the neighbors' kids.

Tuck a love note in your kids' lunches.

Write a thank-you note to an old teacher or pastor or someone who influenced your life in a positive way.

Volunteer some time at a local charitable organization.

Put a ten-dollar bill in a bottle with a note: "Fortune has smiled on you today. If you want to keep it smiling forever, then pass it on." Toss the bottle into a river.

Take a pitcher of cold water over to your neighbor as he mows the grass.

Leave a basket of flowers on someone's doorstep with an anonymous note: "God loves you more than you know."

Say "God Bless You" to three people today.

At the toll booth, multiply the normal toll by ten, and pay the toll for the next nine cars behind you.

Tip the waiter, and ask if you can pick up the tab for some family at another table on the condition that he keep the secret.

Clean the house, and have the table set with flowers and drinks when your spouse gets home.

Compliment your boss today.

Dial a number at random, and tell the person who answers, "God loves you very much." Then hang up.

Send your pastor an anonymous note telling him how much you appreciate him.

Send a note through your child to his or her teacher, telling the teacher you appreciate his or her hard work.

Compliment the co-worker or classmate you like least.

On a hot day, pack a cold drink in ice, and set it out for the trash collector.

Place an ad in the newspaper extolling the virtues of your spouse and thanking God for giving him or her to you. If you can't afford an ad, write a letter to the editor.

Buy a book for someone you appreciate.

Send your child to school with a new pen or fancy eraser for everyone in her classroom.

Have a group of kids put one-dollar bills in helium balloons attached to a note: "The dollar inside is a boomerang gift. Use it to bring joy to someone else, and watch it come back to you."

Pass an encouraging note or a cold drink to the woman at the toll booth.

Take your pet rabbit down to the local nursing home to show the residents.

Shock your landlord by doing something nice for him.

Invite someone to dinner who never gets invited to dinner.

Find a lot where Christmas trees are being sold. Watch for a family who can't seem to afford one, and buy one for them.

Buy pizza for your work group.

Send a check to a charitable organization.

Tuck a love note in your spouse's briefcase, notebook, or pocketbook.

Pray for an enemy, and ask God to show you something good you can do for him or her.

Make several copies of a note: "God wants you to know that you are precious to Him." Drop them in lockers, mailboxes, time-card slots, or slide them under locked doors.

Leave a waitress a twenty-dollar tip with a note: "This is a down payment on wonderful blessings to come. If you think twenty dollars is exciting, just wait until you meet Jesus Christ!"

Pray that God will bring you into contact with someone you can help today; then keep an alert lookout for that person.

Do a task that a co-worker or subordinate finds undesirable.

Buy bagels for the office staff.

Be upbeat all day long.

Call some relatives, and tell them you love them.

Put a note in your church bulletin: For each of the first three people who call me, I will donate up to two free hours this week to be used as you see fit: read aloud, visit, mow, make music, whatever.

Read or tell a child a story.

Say something nice about the last person you criticized to someone else.

Give more than is expected.

Fix something that is broken for someone else.

Imagine you are a contestant in a one-day contest for "kindest person on earth."

Please don't miss out on the joy of being an angel to someone else. It's one of the clearest signs of—as well as one of the shortest routes to—emotional and spiritual maturity. Children start out as takers, demanding the attentions of others. An important part of the process of maturation is learning to give back what has been given; to minister to those who are less fortunate. However, many adults are still spiritual infants who never experience the joy of reaching out to bless others. Indeed, most of us need more growth in this area.

So when you thank God for your angel, thank Him even more

for giving you the opportunity to be an angel to someone else, for it is more blessed to give than to receive. God is watching to see how we use our opportunities to bless others before giving us wider opportunities for service. This life, you see, is just a rehearsal for something far more wonderful to come.

---

1. Kris Coffin, *Insight,* 22 June 1985, 14.

2. William K. Reichard, "I Heard the Voice of an Angel," *North Pacific Union Gleaner,* 2 February 1987, 6.